Water Wisdom: Part 1 - A Journey of Discovery

Copyright © 2021 Robert H. Wellington

This book is a work of fiction. People, places, events, and situations are the products of the authors imagination. Any resemblance to persons, living or dead, or historical events, are purely coincidental.

All rights reserved. No part of this book may be reproduced, distributed, or transmitted in any form or by any means, including photocopying, recording, or other electronic or mechanical methods, without prior written permission from the publisher or author, except in the case of brief quotations embodied in critical reviews and certain other noncommercial uses permitted by copyright law.

Library of Congress Control Number	2021916326
Paperback	978-1-63626-990-0
Hardcover	978-1-63626-988-7
eBook	978-1-63626-989-4

Printed in the United States of America

FRISCO, TX 75034
United States

www.wa-publishing.com

Water Wisdom

Part 1 - A Journey of Discovery

by
Robert H. Wellington

Water Wisdom Part 1 - A Journey of Discovery

Table of Contents

CHAPTER ONE: In the Beginning..1

CHAPTER TWO: What Was That? 7

CHAPTER THREE: The Canoe Trip 11

CHAPTER FOUR: Balance and Baking 17

CHAPTER FIVE: Portage Adventures 21

CHAPTER SIX: Another Day of Magic 35

CHAPTER SEVEN: Thanks for Another Day 41

CHAPTER EIGHT: A Strange Visitor 49

CHAPTER NINE: Time and Eternity 53

CHAPTER TEN: New Breakthroughs 69

CHAPTER ELEVEN: A Small Step Toward Wisdom 75

CHAPTER TWELVE: Wonder..79

CHAPTER THIRTEEN: Indian Petro-glyphs...87

CHAPTER FOURTEEN: Visitors from the Past...95

CHAPTER FIFTEEN: Two Days Remaining 99

CHAPTER SIXTEEN: Back to Civilization..105

CHAPTER SEVENTEEN: Heading Home...111

CHAPTER ONE
In the Beginning

It wasn't that Hall didn't know the answers; he just seemed to have misplaced them. In truth, at this point in his life he wasn't really sure what he had forgotten. He just knew that something deep inside whispered that something was missing and needed to be found.

Hall had just turned twenty-two. A university graduate, his life was full of promise. He had always been a thoughtful person. Even as a kid playing football, he would help the other team's players up after a play, a characteristic that caused the blood pressure of more than one overly competitive peewee-league coach to rise dangerously. He was the first to help his own team's players up as well, which lowered the coach's diastolic pressure and endeared him to teammates and parents alike on both sides of the ball. He was popular but not in an unhealthy sort of way. Rather, he had several loyal friends—men and women—who knew they could count on him, as he knew he could count on them.

In quiet moments he thought, *What is the problem? So much of my life is going in the right direction. I should get on with it—find a meaningful and fulfilling job, get married to a good woman, raise children, and experience life as a family man, neighbor, and involved citizen.* Hall had not overlooked these goals; in fact, they seemed quite appealing. But he couldn't help but feel that he needed to stretch through and beyond a successful and prosperous worldly life to something even more fulfilling, although he wondered to himself what that might be.

Happiest in natural settings, Hall was constantly outside. He loved to go on long bike rides and to hike, canoe, and camp. He especially liked white-water kayaking. There is a hint of danger in the sport, which always seems appealing to a young man still in the bulletproof stage of life. But mostly he liked maneuvering through and with the moving water. Surfing a standing wave, pirouetting after an ender, upstream maneuvers, ferrying, eddy turns, and peeling out—it was all a dance with the water. Fight the current, and you lose. Dance with the water, and you experience something beyond the adrenaline rush.

A little shot of adrenaline was fun too, but Hall wasn't an adrenaline junkie. Upside down in a kayak in a low-oxygen environment is a situation to be avoided or quickly corrected. Fortunately, he had a reliable combat roll and was usually able to throw on a high or low brace to avoid capsizing altogether.

The Eskimo roll is a counterintuitive paddling stroke taken while upside down underwater that rights the canoe or kayak back on top of the water, as it was designed. Hall liked the C-to-C technique in which his body moved from a C position on one side to a C position on the opposite side while executing the stroke. It is one thing to execute the roll in a pool or calm lake, but rolling up while in an aggressive white-water situation was much more challenging. This is why it is referred to as a combat roll, a maneuver that can only be mastered in a dynamic white-water environment.

The Eskimo roll is a heart-pounding part of the dance too. Being upside down in a rushing river with the water's disorienting roar in your ears and your face kissing the deck, as they say, to avoid unseen rocks as you prepare to roll to an upright position, is a surreal experience, providing one with a different perspective on life and certainly a strong appreciation for the simple act of breathing.

Dancing with water in a fast-moving river requires a sharp mind, alertness, and an intuitive sense of nature's rhythm. Much is learned with hours of practice, but those who are really accomplished have a deeper connection with the river and seem to move across and through its features effortlessly and poetically.

Hall loved the water and often reflected on his relationship to it and its effect on him. Water is the life giver. We came from water. Our bodies are primarily comprised of water. It takes little logic to appreciate our relationship to water, but to truly understand it takes a deeper knowing. Whether it is the power of a rushing torrent in flood stage or the quiet serenity of a mountain lake in early morning, water is a metaphor for life in many ways, and as such, draws us to it to share its energy, passion, and peace. We consume it for life. We feel the joy of immersing ourselves in a cool lake or just standing in the rain on a hot summer afternoon. Where there is water, there can be great peace and great passion.

Hall had heard his father talk of these things when he was a young boy and had developed a deep bond with nature. Many days of his youth were spent with his family canoeing through beautiful areas of Canada or hiking mountain and canyon trails. He loved to listen to the wind blowing through the trees and to smell the piney woods. Now in the city, he missed these things. Perhaps this was the emptiness he was feeling. It wasn't that he was unhappy—far from it. He was quite happy and upbeat most of the time. It was just that now that he was forced to think seriously about a career and the mundane daily obligation of providing for his clothing, shelter, and food, he felt a stirring deep within that needed to be identified and incorporated into whatever decision he might make.

Hall had been blessed with a loving family. His mother was quite religious but balanced in her faith. She fully subscribed to the fundamental requirements of a religious life but had a deeper understanding of its secrets and looked past the dogma to the essence, incorporating it into her daily activities. She did her best to teach her children, and more of her teachings were absorbed than her children or she was aware. As they grew older and overcame their rebellious youthful nature, she was rewarded with the surprise of hearing her teachings come back to her from the mouths of her own children.

Hall's dad maneuvered through life balanced by a deep spiritual understanding as well. He called it his compass, but he wasn't particularly religious. Although he could articulate religious points of view, he preferred seeing the truth behind everyday things and especially was at home in nature. He emphasized the spiritual over the religious and spent each early morning meditating and praying. He tried to bring his spiritual life into everything he did but not in a proselytizing way. Rather, he tried to see all of life's experiences with gratitude and forgiveness.

He often said, "If you can see God's hand in everything, you are truly blessed. Such blessing leads to a life of joy whether successful by earthly measurements or not."

He felt that success was in the effort, not in the result. If one did his or her best, the result would take care of itself. This philosophy applied to every walk of life. One need not hole up in a Himalayan cave to find God. Spitit presents opportunities to know It constantly throughout each day, but the true discovery is found within. Hall's dad often said, "The world is healed one encounter at a time. Make each one count. Not only will your life be blessed, but you will also leave a beautiful trail for others to follow."

Hall often thought about these things, but how does one focus only on the action and remain unattached from the result? His dad reassured him by admitting that he was still working on the same conundrum, and although he knew it to be correct, meeting payrolls at his small business and paying for shelter, food, and his children's education sure made results look important. Nevertheless, when he focused on doing his best, the results usually took care of themselves in ways that sometimes surprised and amazed him.

CHAPTER TWO
What Was That?

It was Christmas Eve, and there was an inexplicable joy in the air. No one questioned the pervading happiness, for after all, it was Christmas, but in the back of Hall's mind, he wondered why this year seemed especially joyful. Maybe it was the unusually good rendition of Handel's "Messiah," which Hall's dad set on repeat throughout the day. The hallelujah chorus was especially uplifting. Or maybe it was the full moon. Hall had read that certain Eastern religions gave particular significance to the phases of the moon, and clearly a full moon on the night of Christ's birth must have some influence. But in general, no one gave the joyousness of the day much thought except to connect with it and be filled with its inspiration.

They all enjoyed a wonderful evening meal, and then the family departed to church for the midnight service. The joy of the day carried over to the church service, but during communion Hall felt compelled to pray intensely, giving thanks for the love he felt and had shared during the day. He recited the Lord's Prayer, and when he said, "On earth as it is in heaven," he saw the heavens open up and the multitude of heavenly host descend over the altar, cascading down and all around, blessing and paying homage to all participating.

Was he dreaming? This could not be the result of an overly creative imagination. Hall's eyes were wide open, although he wasn't really looking through his eyes. He was actually seeing the heavens open. The most interesting feeling came over him. It was like he had seen this before. There was a familiarity about it. He didn't remember when, but he had definitely experienced this before.

He heard himself whisper, "There you are. I have missed you."

As his family finished praying and sat back down in the pew, Hall's focus turned to them for a moment. When he looked back, his vision was gone. But there was no doubt in his mind that he had seen something special. He felt a great weight of doubt lift from his psyche, and in its place was indescribable joy.

Upon arriving back at home, everyone went to bed, but Hall felt compelled to pray and meditate. He prayed for several hours and fell into a deep contemplative state. Without warning his body started to shake, from his toes to his head. It was as if every cell in his body had been plugged into an electric outlet. He heard a great wind and felt tremendous pressure in the center of his forehead between his eyebrows from the inside. He opened his eyes, but all was black. He could see nothing, but he heard voices and beautiful song. The pressure inside his head increased, and he felt as if he were being pulled out of his body through the middle of his forehead. Eyes wide open, he saw only black. He had no control over his body. The thought crossed his mind that he might be dying. Never had he felt such indescribable power. He pulled back, thinking he had too much work left in this life to end it here. He groaned with the effort, and far away he heard the sound of his own voice. This provided a point of reference to the world, and he felt his consciousness reenter his body. His sight returned, and suddenly he was back.

Coming to his senses, he sat there with a feeling of great amazement but also regret, for he felt like he had been given a special gift that he may not have completely experienced due to his own fear.

But what was this gift? In fact, what had happened? He had no answers—only a feeling of peace that comes from a deep, inexplicable knowing that there is something more that intimately touches all of us.

Hall thought long and hard about these experiences and realized he needed to retreat from the world for a few weeks to absorb what had happened. Camping trips had always cleared his head in the past. A solo canoe trip might be exactly what he needed. The more he thought about it, the more enthusiastic he became, and he immediately began to plan.

CHAPTER THREE
The Canoe Trip

Hall had been paddling for several hours through the stillness of early morning in Canada's Quetico National Park, one of the premier canoeing parks in Ontario. A cool fog was beginning to lift, revealing a mother duck and her brood scurrying from thicket to thicket along the shore. A Canadian jay could be heard in the distance singing, "My sweet Canada, Canada, Canada; you're so beautiful, beautiful, beautiful." The jay, along with the occasional splash of a fish jumping or the rustling of small animals along the shore, was all that could be heard between the almost-hypnotic, steady splash and pull of the paddle blade through the water.

Hall was a strong man, and each stroke powerfully propelled his craft forward. The whirlpools he created with each pull of the paddle were still swirling several seconds after. Occasionally Hall would stop and just listen. How quiet it became. In such stillness each small noise boomed its presence. He almost felt bad about breaking the calm when he resumed paddling.

It was about 7:00 a.m., and as the sun lifted into the sky, it began to energize the stillness. A slight breeze began to blow, and small ripples appeared where a few minutes earlier there had been utter, mirror like stillness. It is interesting how the sun warms up the atmosphere, causing the ocean of air we call home to begin its daily restlessness.

It looks like I'll have a headwind today, Hall thought to himself. He took a quick glance upward and said, "Thank you."

When Hall was younger, he had dreaded headwinds. On family canoe trips, it seemed like there was always a headwind. He remembered a conversation he'd had with his dad several years earlier.

"Oh no, not another headwind—I hate headwinds. Don't you ever get tired of headwinds, Dad," he used to ask?

His dad would say, "Sure, when I was your age, but then it dawned on me that it all depended on whether you were in a hurry or not. As soon as I decided that I came to these waters each year to participate in the experience they offered and to recharge that something special inside, I began to look forward to any and everything nature was generous enough to share with me. Each moment is precious, Hall. Don't miss one of them."

These words resonated with Hall. From that day forward, he had a different perspective. The wind began to blow harder, and he thought how good it felt on his face. "Just God saying hello," his dad used to say. Funny how such a small adjustment to one's perspective can have such a powerful effect on how he or she experiences life. Life's challenges become treasures; trials become opportunities; moving through the trials becomes growth; and with growth comes increased understanding and the resultant joy of connecting.

It is difficult to handle a one-man canoe in high winds. The bow is constantly being blown around like a weather vane. As the canoe is blown, its side is exposed to the growing waves. This was not Hall's first headwind, however, and he was a skilled paddler.

The trick to paddling in high winds and the resultant high waves was to time one's stroke and roll one's hips, allowing the waves to easily pass beneath the canoe while always keeping maximum clearance between the water and the canoe's gunnels. If one angles the boat slightly, he or she can paddle constantly on one side without a corrective J or pry stroke. In this way, the force of the wind and paddle are balanced, resulting in a constant direction. Again, it's just a dance, but one must remember to always let Mother Nature lead.

Letting Mother Nature lead, hmmm, Hall thought to himself. "Surrender—that's it, surrender to nature, surrender to the spirit. Isn't this the secret to turning trials into treasures?" On he paddled, musing over his latest revelation. Funny how he had been living his life just this way but never realized the simple formula for what he was doing.

He looked out across the lake and saw a small island. *Looks like a good place to camp*, he thought to himself. *About a mile away, I should be there in fifteen to twenty minutes, camping around noon. A little lunch, a refreshing swim, and then some fishing.*

This lake was known for its walleye, the best eating fish in all of the north woods—perhaps the world—and he was going to catch one for dinner.

It was a beautiful island, with a nice fireplace designed with cooking in mind, well located, protected from the wind, and constructed with a large reflector rock. *We will be baking tonight,* he thought. It also had a flat tent site complete with a moss cushion, compliments of a previous visitor, and most importantly a swimming rock jutting well out into the lake. It had just the right elevation from which one could dive and several ledges on the side from which to climb out.

The nicest thing about camping on a small island in the middle of the lake was that there were often fewer mosquitoes. The bad thing about island camping was that sometimes you were less protected from a sudden storm. *Oh well,* Hall thought. *The sky looks friendly, and this is too beautiful a spot to pass up.*

The tent went up quickly, the kitchen arranged, and one or two casts was all that it took to catch dinner—a large walleye pike. There is nothing like fresh walleye.

But first it was time for a refreshing plunge. Hall loved swimming in these lakes, gliding through the crystal clear water. It was as close to flying as he could imagine, and he could swim underwater for more than a minute at a time. A thought of gratitude flashed through his mind as he felt the water rushing over him with its revitalizing energy. Life was truly a gift. Climbing out of the water, he leaned back against a flat rock. His tired muscles relished the sun's warmth, and all seemed good. This was Hall's favorite time of the day when canoeing.

Staring off across the lake, Hall's attention was drawn to the rhythmic lapping of the waves against the shore. He thought about time and how quickly his trip was moving toward its inevitable end and his related reentry into the chaos of everyday life. He was suddenly struck by the silence and drifted far away.

Deep, deep within he heard a song.

Calling sweetly, it was strangely familiar.

Torn between earthly obligations and the song,

Wrestling with daily conflicts, what to do.

Tension between heart and mind,

Praying for awakening to clear the mist.

Knowing in his heart the answer was before him.

Deep within something called.

He had only to choose and it would be so, yet he still slept.

What was it that delayed the morning?

The truth was there.

He would find it.

Soon—very soon—all would be as it should.

A chipmunk rattled something in the kitchen, and Hall stirred. He must have dozed off. He rose with a freshly renewed energy and wondered at his dream. Had he been dreaming? Hardly a minute had gone by, yet he felt a warm comfort as if … He really couldn't explain it, but for some reason he felt like a weight had been lifted.

Hall took out a pen and began to write. He often wrote down his thoughts and was sometimes surprised by the results, but he always enjoyed the effort.

In the Quiet

In the quiet, I grasp your hand,
Lifting me past shifting sands,
Raising me that I might reach
Others trapped within the breech.
Gently spreading light in dark,
Truth revealed within each spark.
A flash, a knowing, sowing seed,
Becoming harvest that will feed
All who stand with arms outstretched.
Releasing pain within their breast,
Replaced with warmth of loving heart,
Replaced with light where once was dark.
And so the cycle journeys on
Until His work is finally done,
Till all are lifted and we find
That no one has been left behind.

CHAPTER FOUR
Balance and Baking

The key to baking a cake in a reflector oven is to spread the heat consistently across the pan so it cooks evenly. The key to spreading the heat evenly is to have a large, flat reflector rock at the back of the fireplace and a fire that was as wide as the oven, but not too hot. Glowing coals were perfect.

A reflector oven is basically two sheets of shiny aluminum slanted at a forty-five-degree angle to each other with a slot for a baking pan usually about eighteen inches long, eight inches wide, and one and a half inches deep. The oven when assembled fits in front of the fireplace. The heat from the fire is reflected onto the pan from above and below.

The tricky part is to mix the cake so it is not too thin and not too thick. Too thick and it burns easily. Too thin and you end up having pudding for dinner, which is not a bad consolation prize but definitely not the objective.

Prior to pouring the cake mix into the pan and placing the pan into the oven, the entire oven must be leveled so the precious cake mix doesn't run out of one corner or another. This is usually done in advance by leveling a pan of water. Although this sounds easy, nature's challenging terrain was not designed with reflector ovens in mind, and the combination of rocks, twigs, or firewood required to level each corner of a pan often results in abstract artistic creations that would have made Picasso proud.

Once the cake is baking, one must watch carefully for uneven areas and stand ready with the trusty tester, usually a freshly whittled twig, that is gently poked into various spots on the cake to see if it is ready to turn. When the tester comes out clean—that is, no mix on it—it is ready to turn.

Another challenging procedure is turning the pan so the opposite side can bake. All this must be done without knocking over the leveling rocks, without burning one's hands (gloves required), and without dumping the cake into the fire. Upon completion, however, there is nothing better than a freshly baked cake enjoyed after a strenuous day in the wilderness.

Hall had baked dozens of cakes in a reflector oven and considered himself somewhat of an expert. The cake was always started about an hour before supper so that it could be cooling on the canoe table (an upside down canoe leveled by a log or two) and the oven would be out of the way when dinner was started.

Hall looked at the cake baking with a certain satisfaction while he chopped additional firewood. The oven was leveled via the support of several flat rocks and one or two small logs. These objects standing alone would appear as random items common to the forest but totally unorganized and certainly not a part of creating a cake. Yet when assembled, they were intimately participating in a creative endeavor. They provided balance, without which the cake would burn or spill. *Order out of chaos*, suddenly flashed through Hall's mind. He smiled at this thought and was reminded of the many unexpected helpers he had encountered, who helped him find balance in a chaotic world. "You never know where help might come from," he mused.

The sound of a splash awakened Hall from his epiphany, reminding him of the beautiful walleye he had caught for dinner. Walking to the fish stringer with its catch by the side of the lake, Hall held the fish up to the sky and said a silent prayer. He thanked God for providing the evening's meal and thanked the walleye for its sacrifice. He had always been moved by the Indian practice of thanking the animal they killed during the hunt and promising that through them the animal would become greater and live on.

Hall filleted the fish quickly and threw the remains well out into a deep part of the lake. Before he could turn and walk to the kitchen to prepare the fillets in corn meal, a seagull landed on a nearby boulder, then another and another. One dove into the water, diving at least twenty feet, and retrieved the carcass. The others soon flew over, and after a brief tug of war, each retired to a separate rock in the lake to enjoy its prize. Hall wondered at God's plan. *Nothing is going to waste this day.*

Hall used waugan sticks to hold two pots over the fire. The waugan stick was usually a green poplar sapling about five or six feet long that was wedged under a rock at one end and angled over the fireplace from the back. One or two pots can fit on each, with plenty of room for a skillet underneath, assuming a properly constructed fireplace.

In addition to walleye we will be dining on string beans and mashed potatoes, the chef thought to himself. Dinner isn't dinner without mashed potatoes. They go with everything, are easy to carry, and give one the carbohydrate boost one needs for the next day. Well, maybe they don't go with fish fillets, but this was a canoe trip. Hall loved mashed potatoes, and most importantly he was hungry—really hungry.

He sat on a rock looking out over a still lake, enjoying a gentle breeze and the smell of pine and a well-earned meal cooking over an open fire after a long but magnificent day of paddling. Well, things couldn't get any better. With that thought, a loon hailing from across the lake punctuated the moment.

Food is always better on a camping trip. Each bite seems to recharge and revitalize the body and mind. Daily toil and nutritious food soon have their effect. Steadily the body strengthens and purifies itself. Like a delicate tuning fork, it begins to vibrate with nature and spirit. As the body becomes increasingly sensitive, the mind likewise is purged of the debris that clouds its vision in urban life and resonates with the joy of participating in life as it is meant to be experienced.

Finishing dinner, Hall quickly cleaned up and prepared the kitchen for the night. The packs and wannigans (a wooden box that carries all the cooking pots, pans, and utensils, with shoulder straps like a backpack, and a tumpline, which is essentially a third strap that goes across the forehead, allowing the neck muscles to carry some of the load) were carefully lined up, covered by a tarp. The food sack was hauled up onto an overhanging tree branch. Nine to ten feet was usually enough. Hall didn't think there were any bears on the island, but they were accomplished swimmers if the prize was tempting enough. It was always a good habit to put the food out of reach of black bears, which are abundant in the north woods.

Leaning against a rock and looking west over the lake, he saw the sun was touching the horizon; a few minutes more and it would set. The sky glowed red, and the water hardly stirred. Only the loon calling to a distant mate broke the stillness. All was good.

CHAPTER FIVE
Portage Adventures

The Milky Way on a clear, moonless night, away from the lights of civilization, is an amazing sight to behold. Shooting stars, familiar constellations, and endless expanses of flickering sky greet their witnesses with a warm hello from creation to the present, sharing their light as if to reassure us that we are not alone. Only a few of the brightest stars are visible to most living in urban settings, but out in nature, Hall felt like he could touch them.

Looking up into the heavens, one is staring back in time to the beginning. Absorbed in their mystery, Hall wished they would reveal their secrets. If there was a beginning, what came before the beginning? If space endlessly turns back upon itself like a giant donut or torus, then what is outside of the donut? Is there only one universe, or are there an infinite number? Does our universe comprise all that God has made manifest or only a small fragment of the total? He had read somewhere that God, the Logos or one consciousness, had created the entire universe with only an infinitesimally small fragment of Himself. Now that was something to ponder.

Hall knew he wasn't the first to have these thoughts but wondered if anyone, either scientist or holy man, had ever touched the answer. If there was an answer, could it be put into words or grasped intellectually? He suspected not, although he was sure it could be known in that realm beyond words, the realm of intuition.

Morning comes early in the north woods. Up at 5:00 a.m., Hall was out of the tent and soon had a fire blazing with kindling and tinder carefully set aside the evening before. Hall put a kettle of water on the fire for morning coffee and oatmeal and began packing his gear and the tent. He brought the canoe to the water's edge and loaded it with all but the kitchen supplies. After a quick breakfast and related cleanup, he was on his way.

Usually an experienced camper can break camp in about an hour. Hall was somewhat obsessive about hitting this benchmark, a trait he rationalized as maintaining tradition and not the least bit compulsive. "Using only one match to light the campfire, now that was compulsive," he said, laughing to himself, although he rarely used more than one and took considerable pride in his fire-making abilities.

As he pushed his fully loaded canoe off the shore, he smiled, knowing he was on his way in fifty-two minutes. Looking back at his campsite, there was not a trace of evidence that he had been there, and he paused a moment to reflect on the island's beauty. He silently wondered if the island had enjoyed his company as much as he had enjoyed the stay.

Hall hoped to cover about twenty-five miles this day. It would be mostly lake paddling, with a few lengthy portages interspersed along the way. With any luck he would be camping by early afternoon. He figured that he traveled at a pace of about four miles per hour in average winds. Headwinds, of course, slowed him down.

Portages, or trails between two navigable bodies of water, come in many sizes and shapes. Portaging is the process of carrying supplies from one side to the other. Today he had two long portages to navigate, a miler and a half miler. To the non-initiated, a mile portage doesn't sound like much. But on a solo trip, Hall would have to make several trips to get all his gear from one side to the other. This miler was particularly difficult because of a hill in the middle and a low swamp, or muskeg, beginning.

I'll take the food pack and tin wannigan initially and come back for the canoe, clothing pack, and tent. With any luck I can make it in two trips, Hall thought to himself.

Portaging on a solo trip is hard enough because of the multiple trips required, but Hall always felt a little uneasy leaving the food pack at one end or the other while he was portaging the remaining gear. His biggest concern was bears, and he had seen quite a few signs that they were active this summer.

On a canoe trip as a small boy with his mom, dad, and older brother, a mother bear and her two cubs had dragged their food pack about two hundred yards over a boulder field and began gorging themselves. Hall and his family had been at the other end of the portage gathering their second load at the time and didn't notice the pack was missing until they began loading the canoes. Hall's dad went all the way back looking for it, about a mile and a half each way, which took almost forty minutes.

While he was gone, Hall and his brother, Kyle, noticed a lot of commotion several hundred yards away behind some large boulders. Being curious and young, Hall and Kyle were compelled to investigate and barely heard their mother's cautionary objections as they flew over the boulder field to see what was going on. They soon discovered two bear cubs enjoying what was left of their food supplies.

They chased the cubs up a tree just as the mother bear appeared from behind a thicket close to the tree. Fortunately, Hall and Kyle had the good sense to back away slowly, being careful not to get between the mother and the cubs. Cautiously they loaded up the shredded pack with what food could be salvaged and headed back across the boulder field to their worried mom. Halfway across they met their dad, who was returning from his unsuccessful search for the pack. He had realized the danger his boys might be in and was charging across the boulder field with axe in hand. He admonished Hall and Kyle for the potential danger they had exposed themselves to, but a slight smile betrayed a hidden pride in his two impulsive sons.

Truthfully Hall had never felt any danger at all. It was only years later that he recognized the possibility of something going wrong. *Was there really any danger?* he thought. *Somehow Kyle and I had a feeling of security backed by some intuitive knowing that there was nothing to be fearful of and all was as it should be.*

They say the young have constant access to God through the intercession of their angels. It is interesting to watch a young child in the presence of fear. Fear is a foreign concept to them. When children fall, they often first look to their mother, whose concerned look tells them whether they should begin crying or if they are okay. It seems that the young learn fear from the world and are not born with it. A thought occurred to Hall that he didn't want to lose, and although he had a long portage ahead of him, he began to write in his journal.

> Fear, such an illusory disruptor of peace; how we let it worm its way inside us, seeming so real and tangible. Like an uninvited enemy, it takes up residence within. Churning our insides, pressing outward on our veins, it works to convince us of the hopelessness of our situation. How utterly dependent upon it we can become. If left unchecked, it soon becomes the motivator of our thoughts and actions.

But what is fear actually but a tense energy in the midsection? What power can it have over us that we don't give it? Redirect the energy through meditation or a vigorous workout and it is gone; reinterpret the energy as loving and we have turned an enemy into a friend.

Fear and related worry fester in the solar plexus, but are they justified? We were not born with them, but rather, we slowly became indoctrinated to them as the pressures of worldly life closed in around our innocent beginning. We focus on our fears and give them energy. Remove the energy and the fear will subside.

But aren't some fears valid—fear of pain, fear for the innocent, fear of death—or is fear merely the manifestation of a feeling of aloneness and being separate? If so, how did we come to this feeling? We must have chosen it, and if so, perhaps we can choose differently. But does it make sense to choose differently? Clearly we are separate bodies with separate minds and thoughts. Rational thought is fully in support of this postulate. How can it be otherwise?

It can be otherwise only if there is something beyond the rational mind, something that binds us and all that exists together, something intuitive, something eternal, something spiritual. If this is the case, than the answer to overcoming fear is right in front of us yet hidden. It is causal and not an effect. It is beyond words because it is beyond rational thought. Each of us was born with it but somehow misplaced it in the chaos of growing up, in the confusion of functioning in a seemingly cold and unforgiving world.

Hall put down his pen, loaded up the tin wannigan, and threw the food pack on top. He was halfway through his trip and thankful that the food pack was considerably lighter than it had been at the start. Thirty steps into the portage, however, Hall was up to his knees in muskeg, basically a boggy swamp. Looking ahead about a hundred yards he could see higher ground, but it was a long, muddy way off.

Muskeg increases the difficulty of portaging several fold. Each step is a labor to pull your leg out of the sucking muck without losing your balance or your boot. Hall was glad it wasn't deeper. For now he was able to keep moving in a steady and deliberate way, but water was seeping over the top of his otherwise-waterproof boots, and he was reminded of the trials of a wet, soggy portage.

Where there is muskeg, there are swarms of mosquitoes, which for the time being were keeping their distance, but it was only a matter of a few more steps before the Cutter bug repellant would sweat off and then they would begin to feast.

Actually, Hall had built up a kind of immunity to mosquitoes after years of camping in the north woods. As a young boy he would get hundreds of bites and scratch sometimes until they bled. But now he would get only a few. He wasn't quite sure why, and he attributed it to a mutated body chemistry. Finally he made it to high ground and began the long methodical trek over the hill to the end of the portage, about another thirteen hundred yards.

Walking with a full load, although exhausting, is primarily excruciating in a few pressure spots. With a pack or wannigan, it is the shoulders, especially the muscles between the neck and shoulders. These muscles usually carry much of the weight and after a few hundred yards begin to complain. A few hundred yards more and they are screaming.

The trick is to periodically take some of the weight off these points, and that is where the tumpline comes in. If you can transfer the weight to a different set of muscles, even for a short time, you can continue to march forward as fresh blood flow refreshes the tired muscles. After the first half mile, one is switching about every thirty seconds but always-moving forward. Hall felt it was actually much harder to stop, unload, rest, and then reload than it was to keep plodding along and switching the weight.

At three-quarters of a mile Hall was looking ahead for the telltale flash of water through the trees. The truth is that you usually can't see the water until you are within fifty yards or so, but on this portage because of the hill, Hall could see the end a quarter mile from the finish.

This is good and bad—good because you know there is an end and bad because it seems to never get any closer. The key is to just keep moving.

The small of Hall's back was beginning to hurt as he reached the end. He sat for a minute, enjoying the sudden relief of unloading the pack and wannigan. He had arrived on a beautiful sand beach, and before him was a lake clearer than any he had seen on his many trips through Canada. It was a sight for the soul, and he took a moment to take it in. This is why he came to these woods year after year. Something deep within him stirred, and for a moment he was lost in its pure serenity.

Time to head back and get the canoe and remaining pack, he thought as he automatically turned and began walking toward the beginning. But a thought flashed through his mind that he should put his food pack in a tree just to be safe, and he turned back. Pulling a rope out of the wannigan, he threw it over a branch about twelve feet high and hoisted the pack up.

Turning again, he was off to get the remaining gear. As he walked back, he mused how he rarely, if ever, put his food pack up in a tree on a portage.

Although a good idea, especially on a solo trip, it was generally considered too much trouble.

Reaching the beginning, Hall loaded up the pack and canoe and began the final leg of this particular portage. He found what he thought was a slightly better way to cross the muskeg and was making good progress when whoa—he was suddenly up to his shoulders in muskeg with only the upside down canoe holding his head and shoulders above the muck. This wasn't good.

He desperately felt for the bottom of the bog, which seemed to be sucking him down as he struggled for a foothold. The canoe was now all that was holding him up. He figured that if all else failed, he could hurl the canoe to the right, where the marsh was somewhat firmer, and use it to pull himself from the sucking mud. But this would also force him deeper into the quagmire and may make escape more challenging or—in a worst case—impossible. If only he could find even a small foothold. He calmed himself and one last time felt for the bottom. His right foot felt something hard. Perhaps this could provide the leverage he needed. With considerable effort, Hall was able to get a slight foothold. With just that little bit of leverage, he threw the canoe off to the side and grabbing its gunnels, used it for balance as he pulled his semi-submerged self and backpack slowly from the sucking bog to firmer ground.

Well that was interesting, he thought to himself. Hall closed his eyes and silently said, "Thanks." He also thought about the deadfall that fell perhaps hundreds of years before and today was his savior. Did it know that one day it would save a trapped traveler?

"Hmmm," was all he could say as he pondered his good fortune. "Maybe I should use the same route as with the first load." Reloading himself, he began again. *If a man swears in the middle of the woods when there is no one to hear him, is he really guilty of swearing,* he thought, laughing to himself?

Safely past the muskeg, Hall began the long trudge up the hill. Funny how he had forgotten how long it was. Sweat was rolling off his brow, and the ever-present hum of mosquitoes was serenading him.

He thought about life and how alive he felt. When he was younger, he had hated swampy, long portages. But he slowly came to realize that this was an experience unique to the north woods, and in a funny way the pain and exhaustion was an initiation into nature's mysteries. Although it took years to come to this conclusion and perhaps it was nothing more than an extreme rationalization, for some strange reason he returned to these woods year after year.

Tipping the canoe forward and then back to move the pressure point where the weight rested on his shoulders, he trudged on. The only problem with tipping the canoe forward to change the pressure point was that you couldn't see where you were going except for a few feet ahead of you. Too many times Hall had met an unexpected deadfall (a fallen tree across the trail), which would knock the canoe back as quickly as it had been moving forward, sometimes knocking it off Hall's shoulders and onto his head with a thump.

A canoe wasn't hard to carry once properly balanced, but if suddenly knocked to one side or the other, it could generate considerable levered torque to the shoulders, neck, and torso. To prevent this Hall would look forward, judge how far it was to the next deadfall, and pick the bow of the canoe up just before reaching the estimated spot. Usually he guessed right, but toward the end of a long portage, fatigue would sometimes impair his judgment. Today, however, he seemed to be on his game and rarely guessed wrong, emphasis on rarely.

As Hall came to the end of the portage, he was startled by the cracking of a tree branch and looked up in time to see a small black bear falling from the tree where he had hoisted the food pack. His black silhouette crashed to the ground and quickly disappeared into the woods. The food pack remained safely hanging in the tree.

Hall smiled. *Amazing, was all that came into his mind. To think how easily I could have ignored the flash of intuition, which compelled me to hoist the food to safety. Really amazing.*

Again he gazed out onto Argo Lake, one of most beautiful he had experienced on his many trips. He loaded the canoe and pushed out into the water. It was the bluest water he had ever seen. The bottom was clearly visible at forty feet. The shoreline was pristine, with granite cliffs and rock outcroppings. Hall hadn't planned on camping here, but this was too beautiful a lake to pass up. Looking around for a campsite, it seemed like he could close his eyes, paddle a few hundred strokes, and beach at any of seemingly dozens of perfect spots. This was a special lake. He couldn't believe that in all his years of camping he had never found his way to this spot.

The amazing thing was that he was all alone. Not a soul was on Argo. It was as if he had walked through a portal to a place that was only available to a few. Paddling to a beautiful point, he put ashore and unloaded his canoe. Taking off his boots, he dove into the lake, muskeg-encrusted clothes and all. Even the water temperature was perfect. Grabbing a bar of Ivory soap, he washed his clothes while still on, rinsed them, and hung them on several branches to dry. The sun was bright, which in combination with a slight breeze would dry his clothes in no time.

Standing with nothing but the skin God gave him, he felt a purity and belonging that few take the opportunity to experience. A line from Khalil Gibran's *The Prophet* came to mind, something about how "the sun longs to touch more of your skin and less of your raiment." Well it was touching nothing but skin today. The wind gently caressed every inch of Hall's body as the sun warmed his skin. It was erotic yet completely innocent and natural. The sun and wind are not the least bit embarrassed at one's nakedness. Rather the experience was more like a mother caring for her child, feeling the beauty of innocence and the need to protect it.

Hall felt frozen in time. He stood until completely dry and then stood some more. He felt the joy of sharing, though nature was his only companion. So much more takes place in life than the senses recognize, but it requires a certain faith, courage, and willingness to experience it. If you let self-conscious inhibitions dissuade you, then you will not share fully in its gifts. If you recognize its reverence and open yourself to it, then life is experienced more abundantly and you find yourself a willing and integral participant in nature's expression.

Experiencing the subtleties of nature's mysteries is merely a stepping-stone to greater secrets that reveal themselves only to the innocent, for these secrets are comprised of pure innocence and thus are recognized by their own, while hidden from a worldly perspective.

Hall was suddenly aware of the sun's heat on his shoulders, and the world came back into focus. His watch said 3:00. It was time to set up camp, but the water beckoned him, and he dove back into the lake for one more swim. After drying off, he put on his newly washed, though somewhat stiff, clothes. They had a nice smell to them, and the stiffness soon softened with wear.

Camp was quickly made, and a large pot of chicken and rice was simmering over the fire. This was Hall's favorite time of the day. Muscles relaxing after a hard day of paddling and portaging, mind clear from fresh air, nutritious food and exercise, and a spirit unburdened from the daily cares and stress of the modern world. It is a peaceful time that is hard to duplicate in an urban environment.

The wind was beginning to pick up, and the western sky was turning dark. *Looks like we're in for a storm,* Hall thought to himself. *Better make sure everything is battened down tonight.* After dinner he wedged the canoe between two trees and tied the bow to one of them. Looking above the tent, he checked for any weak branches or worse, trees that could topple. The tent seemed to be in a safe spot secured between two stout pines. He hoisted the food pack into a tree, and a tarp secured with a few large rocks covered the remaining camping gear.

He could see several angry clouds moving rapidly toward him from the west, and a few sprinkles of rain warned him to get under cover. Entering the tent, but leaving the window facing the lake partially open, he sat and watched in awe as the storm rushed across the water, soon engulfing his small campsite and everything else as far as he could see.

The wind was howling, and the rain was coming down in sheets, propelled horizontally by the gusts. Hall loved to watch nature's fury, as he loved its peace. He thought of John Muir, who would climb a sturdy pine during a storm just so he could feel the storm's power as he swayed to and fro from his lofty post. The trees were bending considerably with each gust, and Hall could hear several snap under the strain. Fortunately he had chosen his tent site well and was not in any danger.

Lightning was flashing all around his little shelter, followed by the booming of its creation, thunder. With each flash, Hall could see outside his tent as if it were daylight. Close by, he saw a family of birds hunkering against the elements within a thicket and a squirrel in the crag of a branch on the lee side of the wind. The wind was howling, and the waves were rolling high over Hall's swim rock where he had enjoyed the sun's warmth just a few hours before.

Hall thought to himself, *How magnificent it all is*. Curiously, he was never afraid during moments like this. Something inside seemed to tell him that he was a part of it, even if only a witness. He mused at the thought of being a witness to nature's fury, somehow safe yet in the middle of it all. His thoughts suddenly turned to the idea of the witness. The Hermetic phrase, "As above, so below," came to mind. He took out his notebook to remember this moment.

> Wasn't the witnessing of the storm the same as witnessing one's own emotional reaction to something? If one merely witnesses and refrains from identifying with one's physical reactions to certain stimuli, eventually those reactions are brought under control, for they are soon starved of energy. That which is observing is the source of all power and energy, and if it merely observes, it gives no energy to a rogue emotion. If it attaches or identifies with the emotion, the energy so transferred causes a reaction in the extreme. This is easily seen in an angry encounter. Feed it with energy by identifying with it and the episode ends in regret; merely observe and soon the storm has passed. Jesus silenced a storm on the Sea of Galilee. I wonder if there is a connection.

With that thought Hall noticed that the storm's fury had passed and a steady rain was falling in its place. The juxtaposition of his thoughts and the recent events filled his mind as he slid into his sleeping bag and slowly drifted off into a well-deserved slumber.

CHAPTER SIX
Another Day of Magic

There is nothing quite like waking in the wild to the sun's rays after a cleansing rain. Hall was quickly out of the tent and breathed in the purified air with a conscious and deliberate passion. The ionized air left behind by the storm energized him and was another reminder of life's perfect balance. Hall thought he might try to catch some fish for breakfast since he needed to let the gear dry before it was packed. He always planned on a few meals from nature's bounty and packed his food supply accordingly. This added a certain suspense to the trip, but more importantly it enhanced the camping experience. Sometimes the fishing gods were less forthcoming than they had been on this trip, and Hall would have to make do with algae soup and cattail roots for a few meals. But somehow Hall felt they were smiling on him this morning. Grabbing his rod and reel and a few secret lures, he pushed the canoe out into the water and paddled to a reef he had seen off a point the day before. Sometimes these little undiscovered reefs were home to a bounty of walleye, northern pike, and bass. He put one of his secret lures (actually it was just a daredevil since Hall only brought a few daredevils of different colors and a few spoons) and cast it over the reef.

He let the lure sink so that he could work it a few feet off the bottom. As he reeled it in—*bang*—something hit his bait with a fury. The drag on his reel screamed as the fish ran. It was a good hundred yards away before it stopped, which was lucky since he was almost out of line. He reeled in as fast as he could as the fish changed direction and charged back toward his canoe. It swam directly under the canoe, and Hall caught a glimpse of a large silhouette as it swam past. Quickly switching his pole to the opposite side, he almost swamped the canoe as he maneuvered the rod, trying not to cut the line against the keel. *Splash*—it jumped in the air, thrashing from side to side as it tried desperately to throw the hook from its mouth. Again and again it ran, then jumped, then ran. Valiantly it fought to escape. It was twenty minutes before Hall pulled an exhausted fish to the side of his canoe. It was a magnificent walleye—the largest Hall had ever hooked. It rolled to its side and looked at Hall for a moment and then slapped its tail against the canoe and tried to run one last time. But it had nothing left and soon tired. As he reeled in and it was again by the side of the boat, Hall was mesmerized by its beauty and its will to survive. He saw that the lure was through the bone of the lip only and instinctively, he reached down, removed the hook, and stroking the fish a few times, he pushed it away from the canoe. The walleye, certain it was still caught, floated there for a moment and then with a sudden flick of its tail realized its good fortune, jumped in the air, and swam quickly away.

"Good-bye brother," Hall said silently to himself. He paddled back to shore, thinking about the gift he had been given. He was filled with a feeling of connectedness, and energy shot through his body. He took out his notebook and began to write.

> What was it that motivated this animal to fight so ferociously for its freedom? What was it that caused me to react instinctively with such a profound recognition of kinship that I couldn't have eaten this proud fish if it was the last bit of food on earth? Was it an evolutionary mutation inherited over the millennia, or was this fire bestowed by the breath of God at the dawn of creation?

Clearly the Creationists would argue one side while Darwinists argue the other, always to the exclusion of the competing theory. But what if they are both partially correct, what if the two theories could find a common unity? Many can't totally embrace a theory of randomness or endorse the theory that God created all at a point in time. But if we look at the mystery from the perspective of a universal consciousness, perhaps there is a place for both theories to reside.

There is no question for many of us that there is a supreme consciousness; something deep inside confirms this to us. Some would call it God, others a higher power, spirit, or source. Just as we long for companionship, to love and belong, this consciousness, which is the motivator of all things, must also long to know and experience itself.

This pull to love combined with moments of inspiration where we recognize our connection to the greater must be tied to a supreme consciousness, something beyond thought and scientific proof, a consciousness that manifests this longing through a creative energy, an energy that tirelessly motivates all forms to combine and cooperate in greater and greater complexity and sophistication such that consciousness can express itself and know itself with increasing depth and understanding.

Thus, it isn't the form that pulls evolution to randomly create something better; it is consciousness, which pulls the form to express its true nature with increasing perfection. Isn't this both creation and Darwinism in one unified theory? Doesn't this explain the historical fossil record more completely, and doesn't this provide a hope for the future as we continue on our journey to understand the meaning of life, a journey that can only be achieved by growing ever closer to this consciousness?

Is this why I let the walleye go? Did I for a brief instant recognize the one consciousness in both me and the fish, this consciousness that longs for expression, to know and to be known, to share and to be shared, to be ever pulled toward its creator like a prodigal son returning home?

Hall put down his pen and pondered for a while. Then realizing he had just released his breakfast into the wild, he was suddenly hungry. *Oh well, I'll have soup for lunch in addition to pilot biscuits and peanut butter and honey. I need to lose a few pounds anyway*, he thought.

Camp was soon broken, and he was on his way. Stroke after stroke he guided his canoe through this pristine wilderness. He drifted away in the silence with only the steady sound of his rhythmic paddling to remind him of his physical existence. Every few strokes he would dip his hand in the water to enjoy its cool and silky touch.

Way up ahead he noticed something swimming across a narrow part of the lake. As he got closer, he saw the unmistakable silhouette of a bull moose's majestic head and antlers. It was amazing how fast he could swim. Its path and Hall's soon merged, and Hall found himself paddling only a few yards from this north woods giant. The moose was swimming at about four miles an hour, cruising speed for a loaded canoe. Hall never would have caught up to him if their paths hadn't converged. It was swimming with a determination, which reminded Hall of his recent experience with the walleye a few hours before. Nostrils were flaring with each breath as powerful legs propelled it forward.

It seemed completely unconcerned by Hall's presence. It seemed unafraid, yet one would think after eons of being hunted by man it would be somewhat nervous. Nevertheless it kept on its course as if entirely alone. It was something to behold, its head, antlers, and shoulders rising considerably above the water with each powerful thrust of its legs.

Hall could see that the shore was rapidly approaching and backed off slightly, allowing the large animal to pull ahead. Hall watched as it neared the shore and began to lift its huge frame out of the water. It looked over its shoulder at Hall and with a snort went crashing through the bush as if nothing was in its way. It bugled to its mate and soon was answered. It was home. All was good.

Hall looked at his watch. It was 1:00. He should have stopped for lunch an hour ago. How long had he been watching the moose? It seemed like time had stood still. Looking around, he found a convenient spot for lunch and began making a fire. Taking out the pilot biscuits, he quickly made two peanut butter and honey treats. He liked to think of them as treats since one has to have a positive attitude to consume pilot biscuits, which are basically giant soda crackers with an uncanny ability to test one's jaw strength. After throwing a kettle on the fire with some broth simmering, he dove into the water to refresh himself. As he climbed out, he caught a glimpse of movement from the corner of his eye. There, standing not fifty yards from him, was the moose he had traveled with just minutes before, still wet from its long swim. A few yards behind were a cow and her calf. Hall couldn't move, not because of any deep-rooted fear but because of the awe of the situation. They looked at each other for a while, and then it moved deeper into the forest.

We're not so different, you and me, Hall thought to himself. And in a moment of intuitive insight, he heard clearly in his head, *No, we are not*.

Hall continued on for a few miles and then made camp. Across the lake was a loon calling to its mate. Not far away was a second male calling. Hall wondered if they were calling to the same female. Their calls were like a beautiful symphony. This day had been full of magic. Several times Hall had lost track completely of time. As he retired for the evening, he wondered what tomorrow would bring. The loons cried till late in the evening, but it didn't matter. Hall was asleep before his head hit the pillow.

CHAPTER SEVEN
Thanks for Another Day

Early the next morning, Hall found himself standing by the shore. He felt the morning sun on his face as it rose over the horizon. Joy expanded within him as it warmed his forehead. A gentle breeze began to blow as the sun warmed the morning air. He stretched his arms to the heavens, giving thanks and blessings for a new day. Slowly opening his eyes, all within his gaze seemed to have a heavenly clarity, a glow from within, that was not usually visible. Staring in wonder, he felt an intimate part of it all. Taking out a pen and his journal, he began to write.

Both Flower and Thorn

Have you ever observed on a sunny morn?

How the light embraces both flower and thorn.

How the breeze caresses all with its touch.

Quaking leaves and pine needles everything such,

That none are neglected and all feel His love.

From the least to the greatest, smallest insect to dove,

Mighty rivers and oceans to dew on a leaf,

All are touched with His goodness, the gift of belief

All encompassed in light, all a part of the whole.
Each an integral player and each with its role.
Only one needs be absent and His works incomplete.
All must be in the picture before we can meet,
The truth at the beginning where we started our quest.
There it was all along deep inside of our breast.
We were lost in a world that we made with our thoughts.
A world filled with comparing and the pain that it brought.
Where there's better and worse, where there's new and there's old.
Where there's black and there's white, where there's lead and there's gold.
He sent light, and it brightened all that it touched.
Laying answers before us, a guide giving much.
Quietly waiting for someone to see.
That the truth is a oneness of you and of me.
And the world of comparing disappears in its glow.
For the light has revealed we're all part of His flow.
Nothing better or worse, nothing plain or so fair.
For we're nothing lest He shines within each to share
Separate bodies we see, separate forms show their face.
But our minds are connected with His holy grace.
So to live life in joy, knowing earth, sky, and sea.
Let truth unfold in you so abundantly,
Pain once falsely embraced, never there, now has ceased.
And your heart now knows love and your soul now knows peace.

Hall put his journal away and began to break camp. He had been looking forward to this day because he had finally arrived at the river and would encounter white water. White water was always an exciting adventure, but Hall usually traveled with several companions, and there was always someone to assist if a boat swamped or otherwise got into trouble. A solo traveler needs to be careful since there is no one but himself to rely on. A thought jumped into Hall's head. *What do you mean there is no one else to rely on for help?*

Sorry, he thought as he looked skyward.

His course today took him through three sets of rapids. When the water was at normal levels, these would generally be considered class III. This year the water was slightly higher than usual. Class III+ in a kayak is one thing, but in a fully loaded, open, one-man touring canoe it was quite different. As Hall paddled that morning, he wondered what these rapids would reveal. The water was higher than usual but not drastically so. Several years ago when he paddled this river the water was unusually high, and one of the hydraulics on the bottom of the rapid had been very unfriendly. Two of the canoes on that trip out of four were caught in it, capsized, and spit out fifty yards downstream. Thankfully no one was injured or traumatized by the incident, and all the belongings were recovered, although the toilet paper was a little worse for wear. In general it was an exhilarating experience that was still the topic of discussion when the friends got together. As Hall thought back on the experience, he made a mental note to thoroughly scout each rapid before attempting to navigate them.

As Hall rounded the bend, he could hear the roar of the first rapid up ahead. He beached his canoe and walked along the shore, checking out each of its features. The top started with a nice V entering into the rapid, with a large rock on either side from which to duck behind before continuing on. On the right was a large but friendly hole (a feature where water flows over a large rock, creating a hydraulic or hole on the downstream side). If the water was rushing fast enough, a large hole developed behind the rock. Sometimes these holes were fun to play in, and sometimes you wanted to avoid them. Usually if the edges of the hole were pointing downstream, the hole was friendly and even if you got caught in it, it would eventually spit you out the side and down the river. If the edges pointed upstream, it was a dangerous and unfriendly hole since the upstream water was constantly recycling you back into the hydraulic. These were the kind of features that can catch an unwary paddler by surprise, exhaust him, and absent a friend to throw him a rope, potentially drown him.

Further down the rapid was a fairly large standing wave. In a covered boat, kayak, or play-boat these waves can be surfed. Standing waves have all the features of an ocean wave except that from the perspective of the shore they are not moving. In relation to the water, they are constantly moving. Hall decided to take it on the left side since it was less violent there, and being an open boat, he was sure to take in some water. So his plan was to hit the V on the left, eddying out behind the rock. He would then carefully peel out and shoot by the left side of the hole. This should line the boat up perfectly to sneak the left side of the standing wave and then hit the pool below the rapids. Hall was feeling adventurous, so he decided to run the rapid with all his gear strapped in rather than portaging it and shooting the rapid with an empty canoe.

He paddled to the top of the rapid, stood up briefly to check his line, and then kneeling low in the canoe, shot down the left side of the V, angling his bow into the eddy behind the rock, which allowed the stern to be swept around. With a little draw stroke he was safely tucked into the eddy facing upstream. *So far so good,* he thought to himself. He looked over his shoulder to check the rapid below him. Everything seemed so much more formidable than it did from shore. He could hear the big hole just below him and thought to himself, *I better hit this right or its swim time.* He paddled upstream slightly and poked his bow through the eddy fence (a five-inch or so wall of water between the rushing V and the lower eddy). He took a stroke, and leaning away from the flow of water, his bow was whipped around and he was heading downstream. *Draw left*, he thought to himself as the large hole revealed itself before him. He passed the hole with inches to spare, getting a good look at how massive it was. *I'm glad you're friendly,* he thought as it roared past. But it had sucked him way too far right, with little time for correction. *Hang on, I'm going to hit the wave right in the middle.* Kneeling low in the boat and with one hard stroke, he was carried right over the top of the wave, taking in a large amount of water over the gunnels as he was carried downstream. With his boat half full of water, he carefully maneuvered it to shore, jumped out, and began to unload and empty it. *Wow,* was his only thought.

The next rapid was uneventful and could be navigated along the right shore with a fully loaded boat. This he accomplished without mishap and continued on to the third and final rapid of the day. This one made Hall nervous. Something kept telling him to portage and not risk swamping, losing his gear, or perhaps something worse.

He walked along the shore, carefully evaluating its dangers and how best to shoot it. About halfway down Hall caught a glimpse of aluminum caught on a rock. As he drew closer, he could see that a canoe must have hit the rock and capsized with its gunnels upstream, and then the force of the water bent the canoe around the rock like it was soft toffee.

That wasn't here a few years ago, he thought to himself. *I hope no one was hurt.* It looked like it would be there for a long time. Hall remembered a canoe trip he took when younger where they started with four canoes and came home with three. Hall got a chill at the thought.

Further downstream a broken paddle had been washed on shore, and below that Hall could hear the roar of the monster hole. Looking at it from a closer angle, Hall remembered why it had eaten two of their canoes on a previous trip. One side of the hole curved upstream and the other slightly downstream. If he had a mishap, he would eventually be spit out the side curving downstream. He would definitely be in the hole for a hair-raising few minutes though, unless he hit the right side just perfectly. *That is just what I will do,* he thought. *I'll hit it perfectly.*

He walked back upstream with that thought in mind, determined to shoot the rapid despite the dangers and apparent intuitive warnings. He portaged his gear and then pushed his canoe out into the stream above the rapid. He quickly stood in the canoe to check his line one last time and then began down the rapid. Angling his canoe to the right of the V, he eddied out to the right after twenty yards and looked downstream, determining his next move. It looked like he needed to move well toward the middle of the rapid to navigate a series of standing waves and shoot past a medium hole just below them. He wanted to sneak the hole on its right side. Having eddied out, his boat was heading up stream. Backing downstream in the eddy as much as he could in order to cross the eddy line at a lower point, he took a hard stroke and maintained the angle of his boat upstream and slightly to the right of the oncoming current so that with several follow-on strokes he could maintain his angle and ferry to another eddy behind a large rock in the middle of the river.

When ferrying across moving water, one maintains an upstream angle while paddling to match the current. The direction of the current zips the canoe across the river at a speed governed by the angle chosen until the paddler is ready to again continue downstream. This Hall did with little effort, and upon reaching the eddy, he gave another hard stroke on the right, pointing his canoe to the left and peeling out into the main current heading downstream. He was on the right side of the standing waves and shot past them without mishap. These waves were sizable at about four feet in height, although not gigantic. Looking downstream at the next hole, he realized he was too far toward the middle and wouldn't be able to sneak it to the right as he had hoped. He would have to power through it. This maneuver was sometimes one's last resort, especially if one was in a relatively un-maneuverable touring canoe in the middle of white water.

Here goes nothing, he thought to himself, and he took two hard strokes, hitting the hole in the middle. The current was stronger than he thought, and when he hit the far side of the hole, the reversing current of the hydraulic began sucking him back into the hole. He paddled with all his strength and slowly, an inch or two at a time, began to power over the back of the hole and out into the downstream current. Hall was relieved, but the big hole was ahead, and it would take all of his skill to negotiate it.

Hall's canoe had taken on some water powering through the last feature. As a result, his maneuverability or what little he had, had been greatly reduced. *This isn't good*, he thought. He wanted to sneak the hole on the left where the edge curled downstream. That way his chances of being spit out were improved if he had a mishap. Without the extra load of water in his canoe, he could have hit it perfectly as he had planned, but he was bogged down by the weight, and maneuvering to the left would only have placed him in the middle of this monster hole. He would have to hit it on the right. There wasn't time to do anything else. He took a stroke to straighten the canoe, said a silent prayer, and hit the hole. It roared as he entered it. Unexpectedly, it twisted his boat hard to the left, turning it sideways in the hole. He leaned downstream to keep from taking in any more water, but he was stuck. He couldn't get out by back paddling because the edge behind him curled upstream and he would be constantly thrown back into the hole. He tried to take a forward stroke but was too deep in the hole to get over the rim even though the edge in front of him curled downstream. This was his only exit outside of swimming, which was always dangerous. If he could just get over the edge. He would have to try to rock himself out.

Rocking out of a hole in white water is like rocking a car that is stuck in the snow back and forth until it is able to free itself. Hall back paddled as hard as he could, trying to get up over the edge behind, knowing that if he could get high enough, the flow of water might be enough to propel him like a slingshot back out the friendly side. After back paddling as hard as he could, he paddled forward. He was right; the flow whipped him high to the left edge, but even after several powerful strokes, he was not high enough to get over the top. He would have to try it again. Again and again he tried. With each try he came an inch or two closer to his goal. "I'm not sure how much longer I can keep this up," he said silently to himself, "but I am so close. One more try. I think I can do it with one more try." With every ounce of his strength, he backed as far up the hole as he could. *This is it*, he thought. With a mighty forward stroke and then another and another, he shot forward. He knew he was close. He would not give up. Stroke after stroke he slowly climbed the last few inches, and then with a sudden rush, he shot over the edge and was free.

That wasn't so hard, he thought, laughing to himself and at the same time promising that next time when his intuition said, "caution," he would listen.

CHAPTER EIGHT
A Strange Visitor

Hall was exhausted. He decided to have lunch at a small campsite at the bottom of the rapid and catch his breath before continuing on his way. He was stirring a pot of chicken noodle soup when he saw him.

There standing a few yards away between him and the river was a curious-looking fellow. He was about five feet tall, with a full beard, long-sleeve T-shirt, and overalls. His clothes were relatively neat and clean for someone who either lived in the woods or was traveling through them. Strangely, he carried no belongings. Perhaps he had a cabin nearby or had flown in on a seaplane for a day of fishing, but he didn't have any fishing equipment either. No question, this was somewhat strange, and Hall's heart picked up a beat.

"Hello," said Hall, wondering how the blazes this strange fellow got so close without him noticing. Maybe he could have snuck up behind Hall, but standing right in front of him with nothing but river and a few yards of beach to approach from was bewildering. "Hello again," said Hall, wondering why he got no response. The man just stood staring at Hall and then the soup and then Hall and so on.

"Would you like some soup?" Hall inquired.

"I thought you'd never ask. I sure am hungry," the man said as he came over grabbed the bowl that Hall had out for himself and dished himself some soup. He sat down a few yards away and began to eat. Interestingly, the man said a short prayer and then slowly and with considerable grace began eating. He seemed to savor each bite. He sat totally silent as he ate. When he was done, he washed the dish, handed it to Hall, and said, "Mighty kind of you, Hall. The name's Joshua, but call me Josh."

Woah, that was too much for Hall. "How do you know my name, and where did you come from, and how did you get so close without me realizing you were here?" The questions suddenly gushed from Hall's mouth.

"Easy, Hall, eat your soup," said Joshua. "We'll have plenty of time to answer your questions."

Ordinarily, Hall might have been somewhat concerned about being in the middle of the north woods where few encounters with other campers occur, much less a strange guy in the middle of the forest who appears out of nowhere, with no apparent camping gear, and who knew his name. But there was nothing threatening about him. In fact, just the opposite was true. The man seemed familiar. There was something about him, a warmth or wisdom or understanding or all of these things wrapped in a form that shouted that there was much more here than what appeared on the surface.

"I love the outdoors," Joshua said. "I thought this spot would be a good place to visit, get caught up, and assist you with your journey."

Hall was absolutely dumbfounded. It was a few seconds that seemed like minutes that the two men stood staring at each other. Finally Hall uttered in a confused tone, "Do I know you?"

"Since the beginning of time," was Joshua's quick retort. "Since the beginning of time."

CHAPTER NINE
Time and Eternity

Hall sat down with his eyes fixed on Joshua. Joshua was consumed watching a loon swim silently in front of the campsite. He seemed unaware or unconcerned that Hall was somewhat shaken by his recent revelation. For a long time no words were spoken between the two. Hall had goose bumps. His whole body was alive with energetic excitement, yet his mind, though totally alert, was peacefully silent. He knew what Joshua had said was true, but how did he know, and what journey was he assisting with? It was all a little unnerving.

Hall closed his eyes and searched for answers. He began to lose track of his unexpected visitor and slipped into a focused state. In the silence he tried to reach a spot in his mind where this knowing that Joshua's words were true was coming from. It were right there, seemingly just out of reach. Silently he sat, intensely trying to reach this hidden place. Finding himself in a deep contemplative silence, his thoughts stopped, and his need to find these memories began to fade. The beauty of the silence was now all that mattered.

Effortlessly he found himself in a beautiful natural setting, familiar yet with an intense light emanating from everywhere and everything. He was next to a river on a campsite below some rapids. There was a fire burning and some chicken noodle soup simmering in a pot.

Wait a minute, this was the campsite he had stopped at after shooting that last rapids. Clearly, it was the same place, only it was so bright and crystalline. Every leaf and pine needle seemed to be vibrating, singing with tones and harmonics he had never heard. The sun was much more intense, but not in a way that hurt his eyes. It played off each ripple of water in the river, flashing a multitude of colors, dancing, warming and illuminating all that it touched. Each reflection seemed to have a conscious life of its own yet still a part of the whole. Hall felt like he was seeing in all directions at the same time. He sat in wonder as he observed all that was happening within his 360-degree view. And that wasn't all; he also could hear all the creatures as they scurried about their business. As he observed, them it seemed like they were acknowledging him as a friend. They had no fear, just a balanced acceptance and connectedness.

It is absolutely magnificent, beyond all words and earthly descriptions, Hall thought to himself. Interestingly, it didn't feel strange at all. Rather there was an intimate familiarity about it. Hall knew this place. He had been here before.

"Beautiful, isn't it, Hall?" Joshua said, breaking the silence.

Hall, somewhat startled by Joshua's voice, responded, "Why yes, it certainly is."

"I thought you would never get here," Joshua commented.

"You have been waiting for me?" Hall asked.

"Well, yes, in a manner of speaking, although the term waiting implies a measurement of time, and time as you measure it doesn't exist here. But as incarnated souls would measure it, we have been waiting for thousands of years," Joshua said.

"This place is so familiar. Have I been here before?" asked Hall. "Never mind answering; I know the answer. It feels like home."

"It is home. This and everywhere simultaneously is home for you and for all of us," said Joshua. "We are the center of all things and the circumference. We are all a part of the one consciousness."

"Only in earthly terms did you ever feel separate, did you ever feel that you could only exist in one place at a time and that all was measured in relation to something else. Only in earthly terms do your thoughts and actions, what you think of as your very being, occur in the realm of time. It has been your job to transcend time, and by joining me here now you have accomplished this."

"I'm confused, Joshua," Hall responded. "It was my job to transcend time—what do you mean by that? And you spoke of a journey—what journey?"

"Fair questions," said Joshua. "I'm not sure I can answer them to the degree that you will find satisfactory, and no one can take your journey for you, but perhaps if we take a closer look you will begin to understand. Time is only one piece of the puzzle but a good place to start. Would this be helpful?"

"Why, um, yes, of course, please," said Hall.

Joshua began, "Although often taken for granted, time is an essential element of manifested creation. In your world of constant action, it measures the gaps between and during activities. As long as there is action, there is time. You measure days by the rotation of the earth, months by the cycles of the moon, years by the earth's orbit of the sun. You have atomic clocks, which measure the vibrations of the atom and relate these vibrations to seconds, minutes, and hours. If one thinks about it, time is nothing more than the measurement of movement and movement must always be the relation of one body to another, from the moon's orbit of the earth to the vibrations of a subatomic particle."

"But Joshua," Hall interrupted, "are you saying that absent movement there is no time?"

Joshua smiled at his engrossed but slightly confused student, and then continued.

"It would appear that time requires movement to exist. Movement manifests as linear, rotational, and vibrational. Some think that light in all its manifestations is the ultimate movement, a constant against which all else in the incarnated world is measured. This is true up to a point. But perhaps there is something before light, before electromagnetism, even before gravity."

He paused, and then continued. "That something is their ultimate cause. That cause would have to create all that exists and govern their position and relation to one another. I would submit that this ultimate cause is consciousness, which unfortunately words fall short of describing."

"But between consciousness and creation there are several other variables about which words, analogy, symbolism and metaphor can begin to describe in a unified, coherent manner. Open your mind and consider the possibility that there is a field that connects everything in an intimate, related, and instantaneous way. Some of your great thinkers have named this field the ether, source field, torsion field, etc. Some even think gravity is the prime mover. There are many ways to describe it, but if you can grasp the concept of interconnectedness of all that exists, you are well on your way to knowing what you need."

Joshua took a deep deliberate breath to let Hall catch up and then continued. "The obvious question, if you follow this line of reasoning is, what is behind this field, this ether, or perhaps gravity as some hypothesize? In my opinion, this is where sacred geometry, the golden mean, and fractals play their essential role. This is wonderfully described by a few of your forward thinking physicists, but I will do my best to present these ideas in an understandable manner."

"If you take a close look at the created universe, you will see the influence of sacred geometry everywhere. In particular, I am referring to the platonic solids. These are seen most easily in crystals but are also present in the building block of life, DNA."

"With respect to DNA, if one were to look down the double helix we are all so familiar with, you will also see the ever-repeating geometry of icosahedron, dodecahedron, icosahedron, etc. A few of this generation's thinkers theorize that this combination of ever-repeating fractal is based on the golden mean or psi, such that charge flowing through it is infinitely compressible and accelerates to speeds exceeding the speed of light. Only a fractal based on the golden mean can do this, and at the point where acceleration exceeds the speed of light, you have life. You have created an environment where consciousness and form can coexist; you have ensoulment."

Hall stared at Joshua with rapt attention. Never had he heard, much less considered, the building blocks of life connected in such a manner.

Joshua continued. "Interestingly, not only is life force connected to the

3D world at this point, but infinite acceleration creates gravity, which brings coherent order out of chaos. Your great physicist, Albert Einstein, related gravity to acceleration and I believe would have been quite thrilled with the notion that acceleration as described previously is the cause of gravity. But then again, I am only a funny character jumping between dimensions as compelled by love. More on that later," he said with a wink.

"As I mentioned earlier, some think the flow of gravity is the cause behind time, but for our purposes, it is enough to relate flow and movement to time, notwithstanding the name others choose to give it."

"So, Hall, we have theorized that consciousness is behind this flow and this flow through and around everything is the prime mover behind creation and therefore time or more comprehensively, space-time. Perhaps an atom is merely a vibrational vortex within this flow. The action of the two upon each other might be the cause behind electromagnetism, and the strong and weak force. Perhaps flow when viewed this way provides the essence of the unified force, the holy grail of physics."

"Wow," said Hall somewhat skeptically. "That sure doesn't sound like mainstream physics."

Joshua paused for effect and smiled again at his student. "What I am trying to encourage, Hall is a stretching of the mind. What I am trying to help you see is the intimate connection of all simultaneously, such that the movement of one impacts the whole in a comprehensive, direct, and also mysterious way. What I want you to see is not only the intimate connection of all, but more importantly your place therein, a place not limited by space or time, but an intimate part of consciousness itself, the cause behind all."

"One might think of the flow of charge as the thread from which the fabric of all that exists is woven. It brings order to chaos, if you will. So flow exists in close proximity to time. In fact, they are intimately connected. They are two sides of the same coin, inseparable yet distinct."

"Throughout the ages your sacred scriptures have supported the existence of an initiating cause, a prime mover. 'Let there be light,' and 'He breathed upon the waters,' are both preludes to creation in the Bible. Similar acts of genesis can be found in most creation stories. But what 'breathed upon the waters,' what was the breath, and what called forth the light?"

"I would submit that consciousness breathed upon the waters, its breath was the flow we just defined, and the waters are the same as the ether or fields, also just described."

"Without creation there is no time, so cause must exist before time in timelessness. That which is eternal is before time or timeless. The soul is eternal, and so it must also exist in timelessness. But as we just theorized, the soul also exists through ensoulment in the created world. Perhaps it is our job in life to connect the two, to bring heaven to earth, to bring His kingdom to 'earth as it is in heaven.'"

He paused again to watch the loon gracefully diving in the crystal clear water.

"But how does one make this connection?" Hall asked. "How does one reconnect the soul incarnate to its higher self? Are meditation, prayer, and contemplation the only way?"

"It is an effective and safe way," Joshua responded. "It is the way recommended and used by all the great spiritual ones who were able to reconnect the lower to the higher. But the universe itself is also currently aiding the world."

"I am referring to the possibility that our solar system passes through a more energetic part of the galaxy periodically and is in fact doing so now. This might explain the bursts of life showing up periodically in the fossil records. A slight but measurable increase in planetary temperatures throughout the solar system as measured by your NASA also reflects this increased energy. As earth passes through this energy, for the next few generations, humanity will experience a quickening and begin to awaken from its long slumber. You are seeing it already, aren't you, Hall?"

Hall nodded as he thought about friends, family, and individuals he had encountered who seemed increasingly aware of reality and the true reasons behind various events.

"You asked about meditation, Hall, so let's address it," Joshua continued.

"The cause is beyond time, as is our true nature. When you pray, meditate, or contemplate, you can touch this state, a state of mind beyond time. Meditation is a quieting of the mind, finding peace, and holding the power of consciousness in a powerful focus. Those who have achieved success in meditation say that time stops, all thoughts cease, and peace is experienced as the meditator merges with pure consciousness, our true state. If we quiet our minds, we are rewarded with the revelation of reality, a reconnecting with our true self."

"Since time stops with the quieting of your thoughts, is time a thought? Thought is movement of the mind and thus a realm in which time must exist. We have already seen that to transcend time we must stop all movement, in this case thought, and we must transcend time to touch the prime cause, our true home, the home of the Father and the beginning and end of the journey of the prodigal son."

"But these thoughts are not new to you, Hall," said Joshua. "You have known them in your heart since the beginning. Remember the poem you recently wrote."

"You mean the poem I wrote on my last birthday?" replied Hall.

In a Moment of Stillness

Another birthday, yet I feel no older.

Another year has passed, yet I am unaware of time.

Time is all about me. It moves through me but is not a part of me.

The world says I am older.

Perhaps my body is, yet I am not.

I am, but not in time.

My body and thoughts exist in time's rhythm,

But I do not.

I hear a different song than the world's, a sweeter song.

It is my song.

But it is also everyone's and everything's song.

Forgive and time stops.

Love, and time is defeated.

But time is not bad.

It has patiently done its work.

It has been my teacher, and it cheers me on as I leave it behind,

For it has accomplished its mission, a job well done.

Now I turn toward home, traveling at unfathomable speeds, yet not moving.

Perfectly still, I approach the Father.

The journey is complete.

In perfect peace I rest.

Looking ahead and to my side, I see the multitudes that have helped me on my way. Looking over my shoulder, I see others following.

A thought of love for those behind instantly takes me back,

For there are stumbling blocks along the roadway that must be removed,

Or at least made visible, that they might be avoided.

There are hands to hold, fallen ones that must be lifted,

Even some who must be carried for a while.

My heart leaps with the joy of giving, even as countless others are helping me.

The energy surrounding my heart, His energy, embraces all who let it enter.

We are not separate.

Time creates the illusion of separateness, but it is only a dream.

Love lifts us above the dream, and we journey on.

It has ever been and will ever be so.

"So you see, Hall, your intuition, which shines through in your poetry, knows all about time. It is just when we get caught up in the chaos of the world that we find ourselves swept up in the world's time trap with its deadlines and illusionary pressures," said Joshua.

"Let's take a moment now and turn to light, time's brother and a first factor in creation," Joshua continued.

"There is more to light than meets the eye, so to speak. All of the incarnated world, the world of three dimensions plus time, is vibrational. The visible spectrum is only a tiny part of the realm created by vibration. Imagine how much of God's vibrational creation we don't fully experience."

He paused to let his last statement sink in, and then continued.

"Imprinted within light's essence is all knowledge without exception. One might say that light (which includes all vibration) is the carrier of God's incarnated message of truth. Likewise, in a very real way God imprinted His message, the key to establishing heaven on earth, on each of our hearts and all of creation. This message is indelibly imprinted on everything that exists, from the largest star to the smallest subatomic particle. Let me try to explain this mystery by using the example of the hologram."

"A hologram, as you probably are aware, is a picture in a photographic medium (usually glass or plastic) made by light (in most cases a high-intensity laser). In a way it is light crystallized in a photographic medium. In simplified terms, a hologram is made by shining a laser on the subject to be photographed and splitting the light in such a way that one beam reaches the photographic medium slightly later and out of phase with the other split beam. Because the two beams or waves are out of phase when they come together they excite the medium's atoms, and the result is a 3D picture of the subject. This is remarkable in and of itself, but the real mystery is that if you break the medium, shattering it into many pieces, there is a perfect replica of the original 3D picture within each piece. The picture within each is not a fragment of the original but a complete copy. It is a fractal, infinitely compressible. And if light is fractal and a constant between all that exists, then the created world must also be fractal."

"The larger pieces require less light to see the picture, but with varying intensities of light, each piece holds a true copy, no matter the size. If you could seamlessly reassemble several pieces, the original picture becomes clearer and clearer with the amount of light required to view it varying inversely with the size."

"But what has this to do with creation, you ask? Well, here is one way to look at it that might help you understand what I am trying to convey."

Hall sat in mesmerized amazement, as Joshua knew his questions before he had completely formulized them in his own mind.

Joshua continued, "If God is light (or at least light is the closest thing we know to God in the manifested universe) then at creation, during the big bang, Vishnu's dream, or other act of creation, when unbelievable energy intensities exploded into the emptiness that became space-time, God's image, His truth, and His word was imprinted onto every atom and subatomic particle created just like the hologram we just described. This ultimately expanded into what you today call the universe. Think about it, God's image imprinted on everything that exists from the smallest subatomic particle to the largest star."

"But what was this message? Is there an easy less technical way to connect with it?" Hall asked hopefully.

"What was the message that spirit imprinted?" Joshua answered. "It has been called many things, but the simplest and most easily understood is *love*. Think about it—love is the ultimate message of one consciousness. Being one with itself, it must attract itself. Imagine a created universe with its trillions and trillions and trillions of particles, each with God's message on it. Each particle must have a natural affinity for every other particle because love must attract itself. Throughout the ages each particle of star stuff with His image imprinted therein has had a natural affinity to organize itself with other star stuff into ever-increasing expressions of His truth and through ever-more-sophisticated forms—from the heavier elements created in the furnaces of the infinite stars to atoms combining into molecules, followed by single- and then multi-cell organisms, to man himself with his conscious ability to relate to his environment and ultimately to the cause behind it."

"The more pieces of the sacred hologram that are organized together the louder spirit's song and the easier to experience it. The universe is, in a very real way, conscious of its creator and is thus able, in the silence, to know Him, their relationship to Him, and thus their true relationship to all. This conscious affinity (which many call love) is Source (for lack of a better term) striving throughout the ages to know It's creations, which are a part of Him, just as His creations have steadily evolved with seeming conscious evolutionary intent to know the Creator."

"Think about the four forces of nature, Hall—gravity, electromagnetism, the strong force, and the weak force. I submit to you that all of these are manifestations of love. Scientists have searched for decades for the one unified force, when it has been right in front of them. It is love. Too often the obvious is ignored, especially by the scientific mind. But things are changing in science. Higher physics and abstract spiritual concepts can hardly be distinguished from each other these days. In fact, the only way one can tell the difference is to look at who is saying them, scientist or philosopher. It is a wonderful thing to observe. Spirit's plan moves forward and will not be denied."

"But I digress," said Joshua. "I'm sure my words sound confusing since the medium of language is so woefully deficient in explaining these concepts of essence. Perhaps if I explain it this way."

"The one constant within the manifested universe is light or if you wish, energy or vibration. It is God incarnate, that which created all, giving each His word and the ability to choose. Choosing Him and the ultimate reassembly of His sacred hologram is the opportunity before us. He is the one constant. We are here to learn to know Him, to realize that we are of Him and as such are not these bodies but something luminous, something reflective of His essence. Thus the universe's natural affinity for itself is in a very real way the expression of love. One might say that the prodigal children of His seed were sent out into nothingness (via the big bang or other act of beginning) to learn who they really are and in so doing, bring spirit's light to the lowest levels of incarnation and establish heaven on earth. Ultimately all return to the Father, after long eons of choices, choices that ultimately transform into wisdom and from wisdom into a perfect image of the Father Himself, until one day one of our own was able to say, 'I and the Father are one.' This is the quest before each of us."

"By joining me here, now, Hall you have taken a giant first step toward achieving the objective of this quest."

Hall, who had been entranced by Joshua's comments, suddenly asked, "Certainly everyday consciousness includes time as a variable, whereas spiritual consciousness does not, with what seems like degrees or quantum jumps between the two. Is time then somehow a path that we can use to gauge our progress home?"

"Very good question, Hall," said Joshua. "All will be answered as you climb the ladder of wisdom. But let me make a few more comments on time that might help point you in the right direction."

"Many great saints from all beliefs have described the eternal as a place without time. Time and its partner, gravity, together seem to be the adhesive, which relates the physical universe to itself. One cannot exist without the other. Remove time and physical manifestation melts away. Remove creation and time disappears with it. If deep meditation is a state of mind, is time merely a state of mind. It has been said that in deep meditation there is only bliss and joy. This is our natural state, which is veiled from us by the challenges of everyday life, challenges directly related to time and deadlines. If time is an illusion of the physical world, and you are able to know this through meditation and contemplation, then it is possible for bliss and joy to take their rightful place in everyday life and bring His heaven to earth."

"Some suggest the pathway to this higher level of awareness is love, and therefore within pure love time does not exist. Without time, aging does not exist, stress cannot be, and joy reestablishes itself within your psyche as the ocean of existence in which you live and move and have your being."

"The formula is simple. We must love intensely and unconditionally. This is difficult for the earthly mind, which exists within a world of judgments and comparisons, but it is a normal state for the heart and ultimately the higher mind, which can be known in deep, loving meditation."

"You might find the following verse helpful in putting it all into perspective," said Joshua.

Before Time

Before time was perfection,
As after time will be,
But during time the soul grows
To know itself and see.
For you have chosen blindness,
Though temporarily
Till you again embrace the truth
And through it are set free.
A choice you made so long ago,
A choice blessed by the One,
His many thoughts sent to the void,
Returning as the Son.

"There is no need for concern," said Joshua. "Spirit's will has manifested already in heaven. The mold is in place, and in your time it will allow each manifested particle to discover its perfection in spirit's unlimited realm. It is a beautiful thing to behold. Each of us is an intimate part of His plan, which can only manifest completely on earth when we each discover this truth and are naturally led to perform our role."

"Yes, we are not only a part of creation; we are creation itself from both a cause and effect perspective. We are not separate from spirit. We are like God's fingers doing His work in these realms. Would you ever say that your fingers were not a part of yourself, Hall?"

"Of course not," responded Hall.

"Neither would God."

CHAPTER TEN
New Breakthroughs

Hall sat in silent thought for several minutes, going over Joshua's words in his mind. The concepts discussed were familiar, but bringing them back to the world would be challenging, for they existed beyond words.

"You are right, Hall," Joshua uttered, reading Hall's deeper thoughts. "Words cannot adequately express any of God's mysteries. They exist in the realm of pure knowing. Ultimately the 3D world is about life and the forms through which the soul experiences it. Perhaps a few words in this area will be helpful."

"Life is everywhere and in all things. When the one cause said the word, it set in motion a vibration out of which creation emerged. From the stillness creation began and continues even today. This vibration is in all things and is the will behind all. From planetary rotation to the movement of subatomic particles, His vibration gives all life. From life's cycles to individual heartbeats, His vibration is the cause and the result of all that exists, seen and unseen. Thus we are intimately tied to the Father and each other."

He continued, "All life has a natural affinity for itself, for it all came from the same source. Truly we have the same Father from the smallest quark to man, arguably the most sophisticated life form on earth (although there are other sophisticated forms), a life form that is a symphony of many smaller parts. We have one source, one song that vibrates through every atom. In that song are infinite octaves and harmonics, constantly expressing source through the infinite fractal of life. We are all brothers and sisters. We are made up of many parts, which come together by this natural affinity of attraction that is His will."

"As life forms became more complex and sophisticated, a marvelous thing happened; consciousness was realized. Of course consciousness was always present, but we were unable to know it in this world until form, obeying this natural law of attraction, reached a sufficient level of sophistication and sensitivity. Again, this natural affinity we know in a higher sense as love."

"Love draws together, which enables consciousness to know itself. One could say that it is this longing to know itself that is the essence of love. God longs to know Himself, just as we long to know God. Love is attracted to love. Beginning with the word, through the chaos of the beginning of time, to the organization of chaos (by virtue of His will and the energy of His spirit, which we call love), we have entered into consciousness, which has as its highest goal self-awareness. Standing on the summit of self-awareness, we know the Father and the Father knows Himself, for both are one. His kingdom has come. The prodigal son has returned home, and God who is infinite has become even greater."

"All is alive and vibrating, Hall, with the song of His first word, which began the cycle of creation. One word and all that exists or will exist came into being. Even the future came into being, separated only by the illusion of time. All that is physical, all ideas, and all knowledge came into being with His word. That which is undiscovered waits only for consciousness to touch it to know its truth."

"Some have touched these truths and brought their beauty down to us that we might know God through their creativity, words, art, and scientific advances. Through direct experience or subtle symbolism, many have left signs, like blazes marking a forest trail, for us to follow until our powers of concentration can know these mysteries directly."

"You know this, Hall. You wrote about it in your journal," said Joshua.

"Yes, I remember," said Hall as he shuffled through the pages of his journal. "Here it is."

> I sit outside looking over a field watching the wind blowing the grasses and leaves of a tree, wondering at its beauty. What secrets each blade of grass holds, even its smallest atom. The mysteries of the universe lie silently in the mere vibrations of the tiniest particle, just waiting to be discovered, calling out to be noticed. A quiet mind and a pure heart hear the calling and long to merge into the ocean of vibration, the symphony created at the beginning of time, which formed all and all are a part of.

He continued reading.

> How many long to move past this world, breaking their earthly bonds and soaring to light and bliss? Some call this heaven or nirvana, and it is the goal of many seeking spiritual transformation. This is a noble goal and so it would seem, but something inside me quietly shouts, "Wait, stop and look around you. Is it the world that binds you to it, or do you bind yourself to the world? We cannot enter heaven with more than we can carry in our hearts. The world is an extraordinary gift from the Father, not a prison. It seems to

me that if you cannot find heaven on earth, you will have difficulty finding it when you pass beyond this life. Jesus' prayer to the Father says, "Thy kingdom come thy will be done on earth as it is in heaven …" But isn't God's kingdom here and everywhere now? How limiting to restrict it to an imagined, other-dimensional location.

Heaven is in everything, for God is in everything and heaven cannot be separate from God, nor can we, and so heaven is in us also. Heaven is loving generosity, infinite forgiveness, and an unfailingly compassionate approach to life. Heaven is revealed through such a life (and lived on earth as well as in heaven) to those who choose a kind and inclusive, coherent life. Do not wish for freedom from this life in order to find heaven in the next, for we are eternal beings and carry our heavenly treasures within us, every step we take, forever and ever. Heaven calls to a loving heart, revealing itself, sharing its treasures, and granting access into its bliss now and today and forever. We have but to look and it is there.

One might wonder, how does one look, and in looking, how does one see? The answer lies within our hearts. The answer is love. See all as beloved brothers and sisters, mothers and fathers, sons and daughters. See the innocence in all, so often hidden by the perceived trials of this world. See yourself in everything and everything within yourself. This is the way of wisdom, which resides in heaven, right here and right now. When the world slings its spears and arrows at you, realize that it is an opportunity to move closer to the Father. Rejoice, for our purpose in this life is to return to our roots, our roots in heaven. Laugh in the face of adversity, for it has no power over you. You can only do your best, and all is for the Father.

The Bhagavad-Gita states, "Make every thought an offering to me, every act a gift to me." That which is eternal knows only light. It is how we perceive the world that gives it its texture. We can choose to see our daily activities as drudgery, or we can choose to see them as a gift.

See all as a gift and the veil, which once blinded you, will lift from your eyes. Perform all obligations with joy and the world has no choice but to love you and to follow your example. Life is so short, and we have so little time to establish His kingdom. Make each encounter count, and with each gift He will multiply them and give them back to you. It is His law. We have only to choose.

"You have hit it on the head, Hall," said Joshua, visibly pleased to hear Hall's words. "Remember that each of us is at a slightly different place on the continuum of understanding leading back to spirit. When we truly hear God's call, our path is a straight line, so to speak, directly to spirit. I can't ask you to come over to my spot and then we will travel to spirit. The shortest way is always a direct line from wherever each of us is. This is why they say there are as many paths to spiritual awakening as there are individuals, but all lead to exactly the same endpoint."

"I like to think of each path as a silky thread of light. Together they create a beautiful tapestry of light between heaven and earth. In truth, awakening is a journey taken without moving, for when we are awake we realize that we are everywhere and always continuously. We are a part of His consciousness, which is infinite. As I said previously, we are at all times the center and the circumference."

There was another long pause.

With the sound of Joshua's last words still illuminating the corridors of his mind, Hall suddenly became conscious of his body sitting in the same place it was when Joshua shocked him with the comment that he had known him since the beginning of time. As his eyes came back into focus, he saw Joshua looking out over the river, still mesmerized by the loon swimming in front of the campsite. It was as if time had stood still. The loon had barely moved from the last time Hall had noticed it. Had he really had a deep discussion on time and life and heaven on earth with Joshua, or was it a dream?

"Well I'll be off," said Joshua. "Just remember that you are always surrounded and penetrated by infinite love. And one final thought—when the world around you appears hopelessly lost, surround it with your love and continue your dance. The rest will take care of itself."

With that and before Hall could utter a word of protest or even thank you, he was gone.

Hall quickly loaded his canoe and pushed out into the river. It was funny. He didn't really feel like Joshua had left. It was more like he was right there with him as he had always been. He was beginning to remember.

CHAPTER ELEVEN
A Small Step Toward Wisdom

Paddling past beautiful cliffs with just enough current to make the journey effortless, Hall felt like he was still in the contemplative state he had been when discussing time with Joshua. It was like he had brought the light from that higher awareness back down with him. All was a little brighter, with perfect contrast, like a vast crystal paradise of infinite color. Perhaps this was some of what establishing His kingdom on earth was all about?

For now he would just enjoy the moment. He was filled with energy. He observed everything happening along the shore, in the air, and on the river. He noticed he was smiling from ear to ear. When he temporarily became conscious of it, it would fade, but within a short while it was back on his face. He felt like all was perfect, with nothing out of place. It was as it should be.

He was about to burst with happiness when he spontaneously pulled his canoe to the shore and onto a small beach next to one of the cliffs rising straight up from the water's edge. He got out and began climbing. He needed to jump off one of these cliffs. It wasn't clear why; it just seemed right. They were too beautiful, and he felt too good to miss such an opportunity.

This had been a custom on many a canoe trip since he was a small boy. In his youth he was often petrified, as his fellow campers would urge him on from their canoes as he stood on the precipice looking down at them. They had already jumped while Hall was still getting up his nerve. It was about a fifty-foot cliff, and it seemed like a long way down, especially viewing the jump from the top. Somehow it always looked higher from the top than from the bottom. It was a hot day, and Hall was fully clothed, although he had left his hunting knife, compass, and other pocket camping paraphernalia in the canoe. He usually jumped with his boots on, and today would be no exception. They cushioned some of the sting from the water upon entry but truthfully were also absolutely necessary for the climb.

He climbed to the top and looked for a good spot to jump from. The water was quite clear, and he could see several places deep enough to jump safely. Just a few feet to his right was a rock promontory that would be a perfect place from which to leap. He worked his way to its edge and gazed at the amazing view before him. He could see for miles down the river and even beyond to a few lakes in the distance. He thought he saw a cow moose and her calf across the river, moving along the shore. It was a moose, and as he watched, it slowly moved back into the forest.

Then he looked down, and something gripped his stomach like a vise. It was the same fear he used to experience as a child when facing a jump like this. These kinds of jumps usually petrified him, but always he pushed through it and jumped anyway. Here was that fear again, an old friend come to pay a visit. Instead of pushing past it with pure willpower like in the past, this time he just observed it. He hadn't felt this fear in years, not since the last time he was standing on a cliff about to jump. Where had this fear been hiding all this time? Frankly, when Hall pulled to shore to climb the cliff, he had been so caught up in the moment that he was oblivious to any fear. Now here it was again, right on queue.

Interesting, Hall thought to himself. While Hall was observing the fear, he noticed something different. The knot in his solar plexus was subsiding. It dawned on him that by observing the fear as opposed to identifying with it, he gave it no energy. In fact, he was totally separate from the fear. He was the observer. Only by identifying with it could it drain his power. It was being starved of its energy supply, and it was disintegrating before his mind's eye. Suddenly, with an imagined pop, it was gone. Hall stood up, took a deep breath, and launched himself into the air and over the cliff. For the first time, he was actually enjoying the ride down. In the past it seemed like an eternity before he would hit the water. This time he felt like a bird, gliding effortlessly. It was a feeling of freedom like he had never felt.

Splash, his feet hit the water, and his body submerged. With an incredibly pleasant suddenness, every square centimeter of his body was cooled and refreshed. He took a couple strokes and rose to the surface. Swimming to the beach where the canoe was, he thought about what had just happened and quietly whispered, "Thanks." Five jumps later, he was again on his way.

CHAPTER TWELVE
Wonder

Hall woke the next morning wondering if the prior day had actually happened. He knew from the map that he had traveled about twenty-five miles, but the day was filled with such magic it almost seemed like a dream.

We'll have oatmeal with raisins and brown sugar, along with hot chocolate this morning, he thought to himself with a smile. He was smiling because this is what he had every morning, although sometimes he substituted cream of wheat as a special treat. Somehow on a canoe trip, you never got tired of it. At home one could have oatmeal for about two days before desperately seeking something new for breakfast. The tent was down quickly, breakfast dishes cleaned and put away, and the canoe loaded.

It was another beautiful, sunny day. There had been some rain, enough to remove most of the fire hazard, but this had been at night. Rain at night provided a gentle white noise against the tent and usually resulted in an amazing night's sleep. Hall was about to push out into the river when he got an urge to take out his journal and record his thoughts. He was never quite sure what he would write about but was usually pleased with the result. To him it was a creative process; one had to let it unfold before one could witness the full bloom. When no thoughts came to him, he would merely close his eyes and enjoy the moment. Almost always an inspiration would come through and he would begin to write.

Wonder

The wind whispering through the leaves
causes me to stop in wonder.
A forest stream, sometimes roaring with winter's thaw, sometimes a gentle trickle, calms my soul.
Sunshine working its way through the forest's canopy, flickering upon the ground,
speaks to something deep within.
The beauty of a pristine northern lake sparkles in His infiniteness.
I watch as wind, waves, and sunlight dance together.
All are wonders that hold the answers to a great mystery if we take the time to observe and listen.
All are a part of us as we are a part of everything.
The power and majesty of nature's wonders greet us as brothers and sisters.
Joy explodes within as we recognize our kinship.
Man and nature created through the one will
for each other's pleasure.
Listen to nature's song and begin to tap life's abundance.
Know that the wind is caressing us as it moves past,
That the sun warms us and lights our way with the joy of a mother looking over her children.
Know that the waters cleanse, cool, and nourish us with a conscious joy.

> There is no limit to nature's sharing,
>
> for in sharing it completes itself,
>
> just as we are completed by sharing.
>
> The wonder of life is His gift.
>
> We have only to reach for it and He will place it gently in our outstretched hands.

Pushing off into the river, Hall paddled with anticipation of what the day would bring. This was the last day of river travel, followed by a few days of lake paddling before being picked up by the seaplane that would bring him back to civilization. The thought of leaving God's wonderland usually saddened Hall. This had been a magical trip, full of wonder, small and large revelations and growth. He didn't want to leave it behind, but somehow he felt in the deep recesses of his mind that this time it would be different. This time he would bring the peace and serenity of the wilderness back with him. This time it would be his constant companion, wherever he was and whatever he was doing.

Catching himself musing about the future, he resolved to enjoy every last moment, in the moment. His experiences and growth, even his very soul was in the moment. Staying in the moment now and a few days from now back in civilization, even the rest of his life, wherever it might lead, that was the secret and the magic.

There was something special about this day. There would be no rapids, but the current moved along at a steady two to three miles an hour, and the canoe seemed to effortlessly glide forward. Around every corner was a surprise. Beautiful cliffs rose up along the shore. Interspersed between these majestic outcroppings was a dense forest of pine, cedar, poplar, and birch. Every few miles a stream would meander to the river's edge, and moose, beaver, water fowl, and the occasional jumping fish could be seen by the alert traveler. The steady rhythm of the paddle and gentle flowing of water under Hall's canoe put him in a contemplative state. There was a joy in each stroke, time stood still, and every few minutes Hall found himself in a timeless wonderland interrupted only by the slap of a beaver's tail or sudden gust of wind. He was totally tuned in to the moment. It seemed like he could see the leaves and pine needles exhaling their life-giving oxygen that was carried to him by the breezes. With each breath he consciously returned the favor and for a moment thought he caught them smiling at him. He had forgotten about the chaos of the city and only knew the peace of the moment. He focused on the steady rhythm of his breathing, consciously aware of its power as he inhaled and the gift of light as he exhaled. He thought of nothing else, for he did not want the moment to ever end. Even the waves spoke to him as the sun danced on each ripple. Water broke the light into a million flashes, each singing a note in nature's symphony. One source of light, yet millions of expressions when the two come together.

He thought about the relationship of life and water, spirit and light. He thought about himself as one of these expressions of light and his relationship to all men and all of creation. It was so clear out here in the wilderness. Would he be able to bring this undeniable feeling of oneness back to the bustling crowds of civilization? Could he walk in peace through chaos? Something deep inside answered with a resounding yes. Somehow he knew he would be able to.

Strangely, but without effort, something had opened in him during this journey through wilderness, something magical and mysterious, something beyond words but absolutely undeniable. He was aware of every tree, every leaf and pine needle. Wildlife he passed acknowledged him as a brother and even went out of its way to be seen by him. The very rocks seemed to vibrate as he passed.

Rounding a bend, the river opened to a beautiful lake. About two miles out was an island with a beautiful granite outcropping and gentle slope to the water. Hall suddenly realized he was at the day's destination. He couldn't be here already, he thought. The day was to include thirty miles of river paddling. He hadn't even stopped for lunch.

With that thought, he became aware of a healthy hunger in his midsection. He realized that indeed he had traveled the thirty planned miles and indeed he had missed lunch. He pondered the timelessness of the day and found himself paddling with an extra vigor as thoughts of food played in his mind. Beaching the canoe at the island's edge, he unloaded his packs and looked for a tent site. There were several to pick from, but he selected one with a westerly view overlooking the lake.

Tonight we feast, he thought to himself, wondering who we might be and mused of Joshua halfheartedly.

"Did someone say feast?" a voice behind him called. Turning, Hall saw the familiar figure of Joshua sitting on a boulder near the fireplace.

"Don't you ever knock?" Hall joked.

In truth Hall was quite happy to see him and even felt a surge of energy as he contemplated the possibilities for tonight's discussion.
"There are ripe blueberries on the far side," Joshua commented as he grabbed a small pot and headed across the island.

"Then blueberry pie it is," Hall answered on cue.

Hall cut some wood and quickly had a fire started. He kneaded some dough and carefully rolled it out on the bottom of the canoe table. Leveling the reflector oven and greasing the pan, he laid the soon-to-be crust in the pan's bottom and baked it for a few minutes until it became brown and flaky. As he finished, Joshua returned with a full pot of blueberries. They were fresh, plump, and sweet. Hall added a little sugar and water to the pot and began cooking the berries. Rice was boiling in another pot, as were some freeze-dried beans and a can of chicken.

When the blueberries had fully cooked, Hall poured them into the oven pan and laid slices of pie crust in a crossing pattern over the top. The pie was placed in the reflector oven for a few minutes of baking while the chicken and rice was dished for Hall and Joshua.

Hardly a word had been spoken, yet Hall and Joshua worked in total coordination with each other. They each took a dish, found a comfortable rock to sit on, said a short prayer of thanks and ate. Hall hadn't had food this good in a long time. Each bite was a ceremony of thanksgiving. He felt the energy surge through him as he finished. Both he and Joshua got up, washed their dishes, and walked to where the pie was cooking. It looked magnificent. Two pieces of pie later the kitchen was put away for the evening. Joshua and Hall sat looking out over the lake at the crimson rays of the sun as it set.

"Quite a day today, wasn't it, Hall?"

"Quite a day indeed," was the response. "I blinked and it was over, yet I remember each intimate moment as if it spanned a millennium. Today seemed like a watershed, a new beginning. I have often dreamed of such days. Today dreaming and reality merged. And it hasn't ended. I don't think it will end. Rather I think it is an awakening. It is clear to me now that I have been dozing. I feel a new power and with it a new responsibility. I can't stand the thought of others sleeping, unable to experience reality, thinking they are separate, different, unworthy, and helpless in a seeming unjust existence. I feel like I am about to explode with compassion for each of them. I need to share these things. I need to help."

"And so you shall," said Joshua. "But remember, you can't live someone's life for him or her. Each must make the choice to wake up. It is available to all. Each person has only to respond to the song you heard long ago. Hall, remember always that you are not alone; thousands are working alongside you. Many are fully conscious of their roles; some are living their purposes without total awakening, and some cannot yet be seen by you. Things are accelerating. We are approaching the time of new beginnings. Many have heard the song and are emerging from slumber."

"But there are those who will resist. There are those content in the status quo, who, because of some underlying fear or an overwhelming need for wealth or power, will resist the song. Look around you. Increasingly the message you see in the press, television, or other media is negative and designed to produce fear, a fear that enables those in power to remain in power. Wars, pestilence, plague, terrorism, religious bigotry, crime, environmental disasters—the list goes on and on."

Joshua paused for a moment to let Hall think. He continued, "Sadly, some have chosen to contribute to this darkness, sometimes consciously and sometimes unconsciously. Always they act from blindness. It has been so for thousands of years. But now it is time to awaken. It is not hard. It requires looking in a place unfamiliar to most. It requires looking within."

"Unfortunately, even those who look within must first clear the sludge deposited in the psyche of humanity over a millennium, before they begin to see the glow of who they really are, of their royal heritage and connection to all. Your job, Hall, like all who have rekindled their light within, is to love them. Follow your heart and you will be fulfilling your purpose. Some will seek guidance. Some will feel the love you share. Others may only begin to turn their heads toward some mysterious melody. Some will hate you, but not know why. Despite their actions or reasons, your love will be enough."

"Hall, I came to you because you called. In time others will call to you and you will respond. As more regain their sight and more light is set free upon the world, the awakening will accelerate. Stay the course. The seeming darkness can only be overcome by light. God bless you. You are never alone."

Hall closed his eyes as Joshua spoke in an effort to absorb his message fully. When he reopened them, Joshua was gone.

CHAPTER THIRTEEN
Indian Petro-glyphs

Another morning in God's country. "Daylight in the swamps," his dad used to say to roust Hall and his siblings out of the tent on family canoe trips.

Cooking breakfast, breaking camp, and getting underway to another day of traveling was completed with Hall's usual efficiency. Somehow he never got tired of the mundane when he was camping. When done properly, it is a process requiring participation and coordination of body, mind, and soul. Every movement seemed connected to every aspect of the experience, sights, sounds, smells, and thoughts. Several days in the woods did something to a person. It cleans one on all levels.

Today Hall planned about twenty miles of paddling and portaging, about a four- or five-hour effort in a one-man fully loaded canoe. The weather had been perfect the entire trip; sun during the day and when it did rain, it was in the evening where the rhythmic sound of raindrops on the tent soothed the traveler into deep, healing levels of sleep. Hall was feeling life and the wonder of creation physically, emotionally, and spiritually. His intuition, unhindered by the chaotic energy of urban living, had expanded. It was like an old friend had returned, for the feeling was as natural as breathing.

Each day he felt more alive than the day before. Jesus had said that He had come to teach men how to live life more abundantly. Hall thought he was beginning to glimpse some of the meaning behind those words. The wind was fresh, the breeze touching his face and arms like a loving mother. The light played off each pine tree, leaf, rock, and wave such that all seemed connected to him. Even the cool water on his hand as he dipped his paddle was in communion with him.

He felt a palpable exchange of energy with his surroundings, always receiving more than he gave, and yet the flow was dynamic and infinite. Although the flow was always present to some degree, his conscious awareness of it increased the exchange, and he felt a palpable joy. He observed himself holding back on the feeling and thought to himself, Why? He heard an inner voice say, "Don't hold back. Let it flow. Send it to all your loved ones and to all that exists, visible and invisible."

It dawned on him that holding back his joy was somewhat familiar, as one observes a bad habit for the first time. *Have I been holding back all these years,* he thought to himself? *Why? What am I afraid of? Why would I hold back on this feeling, this energy, which today I recognize as nothing less than my true nature expressing itself within an infinite consciousness?*

Hall continued his steady paddling, pondering his mini epiphany. He was experiencing something beyond himself, something that had always been there, waiting to be discovered. He wondered if he would be able to maintain this awakening, this present moment, this now.

Suddenly he realized he was in a canoe again, that his left shoulder was sore and he needed to change sides paddling. His stomach growled that lunchtime was near and that he still had a ways to go. The joyful energy had subsided, and his thoughts flashed between how far he had traveled that day and how much canoeing remained. After feeling so fulfilled, he suddenly felt tired and wished for the day to be over. *What happened?* he thought. He longed for the joy he had recently experienced and wondered why it had been so fleeting.

He stopped paddling, closed his eyes, and listened to the wind. It was calling to him. He became aware of waves of joy flowing through him again. He silently said, "Thank you," and felt immediate rushes of energy and accompanying goose bumps on his arms and a tingling on his head. It was suddenly clear to him. He was back in the very present state of a few minutes earlier. This was his natural state, a state of infinite possibilities and connectedness. Strangely, he had lost the state when he worried about losing it.

One has to be the state to be in it. Worrying about losing it puts one back in the past or the future but not the present. True consciousness is in the present and only the present. Fretting over past actions or worrying about the future, disconnects one from the present. When we are disconnected from our true state, a longing for something missing becomes our state.

This usually manifests into various levels of depression and/or anxiety. Hall thought of the enormous sales of Prozac, Zoloft, and other antidepression/antianxiety medications and felt an overwhelming compassion for those compelled to use them. His compassion throbbed for those caught in the web of drug dependency, legal and illegal. There must be a way he could help. There must be a way to share his discovery.

Pondering this thought, he paddled on. Up ahead were several cliff paintings, petroglyphs, left by travelers a few hundred or perhaps a few thousand years earlier. Hall had seen these paintings when a small boy on one of the many canoe trips his family took each summer. They were partially hidden in a cove, which was dry and offered a perfect location to put ashore, camp, or just stop for a meal. Hall wondered if he would recognize the spot, for it was no longer marked on the map for historical preservation reasons. It seemed too many passers-by wanted the pictures for their private collection or as an interesting inlay built into their fireplace and often would try using hammer or other available tool to bring one or more petroglyphs home. Hall saw a rock formation that looked strangely familiar about two to three miles across the lake and headed in that direction.

It was a beautiful day, and Hall was enjoying an almost perfect tailwind. To a canoeist it seemed that wind and headwind were synonymous terms. Hall, in fact, was partially stunned by the fortunate and unexpected tail wind and pulled to the near shore to cut two small saplings to be used as masts. He wedged the saplings between the thwart brace and tin wannigan after tying a small tarp between them. He also tied two lengths of nylon cord from his seat to the top of each sapling to stabilize his makeshift sail. He pushed back out into the lake, and using his feet to hold each sapling base in place and his paddle as a rudder, he began to sail. Usually on a multi-canoe excursion, there were plenty of people to hold and stabilize the sail, which was a large tarp spread across three to four canoes. Hall wondered if he could handle both sail and rudder by himself if he encountered a large gust. *Here goes*, he thought.

Hall estimated it was just under three miles from his present location to the cliffs. Paddling such a distance would take an hour or so. Hall thought that given the wind conditions, he could probably sail at about the same pace as he could paddle, and he leaned back on one of his packs and began to enjoy his effortless journey. All was well until about halfway across the lake when the wind picked up considerably. Hall had been lulled into a daydreaming state when a gust caught full by the sail pushed hard on Hall's feet that he had been using as leverage against the sapling masts to keep them upright. The canoe surged forward. Hall looked behind him and realized that he was leaving a considerable wake. He was flying, and it was all he could do to keep the canoe straight as it caught up with the swells and surfed for a while on each as it passed.

"Yahoo!" Hall heard himself say.

The canoe was traveling at such velocity that the water was almost up to the canoe's gunnels. Looking ahead he realized that he had already crossed the lake and the cliffs were rapidly approaching. Releasing the base of the masts, the sail was blown flat against the front of the canoe, but part of the sail fell into the lake and began to fill with water. Hall needed to release the nylon stabilizing cords tied to his seat before the filling sail swamped his small boat, but they were too tight to untie easily in the wind and swells. Quickly he removed his knife from its sheath and with one movement cut both cords close to the seat where they were attached. The canoe, which was leaning, heavily to one side, immediately righted itself, and the tarp and two saplings fell harmlessly into the water next to the boat. With some effort Hall maneuvered the canoe so that he could untie and gather the tarp as well as the cord still tied to the top of the mast.

The two saplings remained in the lake and in time would find a distant shore. Perhaps they would eventually be buried in a muskeg bog waiting to help an unwary traveler. Hall smiled at the thought and again said a silent thanks for his rescue a few days earlier.

He had taken in some water and scanned the island's shore in front of the cliffs for a good place to beach and empty his canoe. To the left and slightly hidden was what looked like a small inlet. Hall paddled into it and beached his canoe on a beautiful sandy spot just out of the wind. *Wow, that was some ride. It is amazing how quickly conditions can change,* he thought to himself.

Still the experience seemed well worth the risk, although if Hall had realized how much the wind would pick up at this end of the lake, he might have thought differently about the joys of sailing in a one-man canoe. Hall emptied his canoe, repacked it, and was about to push out into the water when he took a moment to look at the cliffs that surrounded him. He had completely forgotten about the petroglyphs, but there they were, right in front of his eyes. There were dozens of them. Clearly, history's travelers had visited this place many times and during different water levels, for the paintings were of several different styles and at all levels, from just below the water line to levels that today would require a ladder to reach.

Generally they were reddish, but black or dark gray were also visible. There were pictures of animals encountered or hunted, bear, deer, moose, and either dog or wolf. There was a man holding a large fish. There were hunting parties depicted, bows and arrows and spears. A large bird resembling an eagle was shown, and it had what appeared to be a fish in one of its talons. There were handprints interspersed throughout the other paintings, perhaps an artist's signature. Hall lay on his back gazing at the history and stories in front of him, painted over the millennia by those who came before. Some were quite artistically drawn, while others were more like the stick men paintings of Halls childhood, but all told a story from the unique perspective of the artist.

Hall wondered if a hunting party would leave the women and children behind during an excursion and whether the children would draw on the rocks, much as kids do today with paper and crayons. Some had a certain sacred energy about them, and others were probably nothing more than ancient graffiti. One set of pictures showed hunting parties carrying a deer back to camp tied on a stick carried between two men. All the hunters were definitely male, although some were depicted more male than others. Hall mused if this symbolically depicts the hierarchy of hunting prowess between the participants or was it merely an opportunity for the artist to present himself a little larger than life. It didn't really matter; Hall chuckled at the thought of running through the thick underbrush if the paintings were anything more than symbol.

Hall had an affinity for these people. They seemed so real, so human, like they were still there. Hall smiled, lifted his arms to the sky, and gave thanks for this remarkable day.

Rather than continue on, as had been his earlier plan, Hall decided to spend the night here under these cliffs. There were plenty of good tent sites as well as rocks to construct a fireplace and kitchen. So he set to work unloading the canoe, and in no time camp was set up. As was his custom when the work was done, it was time for a swim. Hall swam to the cliffs so he could take a closer look at the paintings. There was a small ledge just underwater that he could stand on while he examined the pictures more closely. It was amazing. He felt like he was on sacred ground. Upon close examination he could see generations of pictures, some quite faint and apparently painted over. Others were bold, standing out like they had been painted only yesterday.

All these rocks are part of the Canadian Shield—some of the oldest rocks in the world, scraped clean by the glaciers thousands of years ago, a huge granite formation stretching across much of central Canada. There was no telling how old the paintings were, but it was clear that many were ancient.

This was a special place, a different place than Hall remembered from his childhood. It was not an obvious inlet from out on the lake, and Hall surmised that most travelers probably paddled right past it on their journey. But somehow Hall had found it. The wind had brought him here and he felt a shiver at the thought. For some strange reason, Hall knew that he was supposed to be here.

CHAPTER FOURTEEN
Visitors from the Past

Rice, chicken flavored textured vegetable protein, or TVP, as it was affectionately known during his younger camping days, and freeze-dried vegetables were the evening fare. The fireplace did not have a suitable reflector rock, so there would be no baking tonight, but Hall had some butterscotch pudding left so all was well on the dessert front. To drink, Hall planned on cherry bug juice (lemonade). It was going to be a feast. Actually every night was a feast as hungry as one gets on a canoe trip. Hall opened the TVP and began to soak it in lightly salted and boiling water. It would be a good hour before it was ready to be added to the chicken stew mix. TVP that wasn't cooked sufficiently would bounce like a small super ball if it fell off your plate and could easily wear out a set of molars trying to chew it. TVP is essentially a soybean product, packed with protein, yet is quite light and easy to carry in a dry state. There were better products today, but Hall liked to pack TVP in memory of his childhood and teenage camping trips.

The sun was behind the cliff, and although it was not yet dusk, it was getting dark in this hidden cove. Hall decided to add a few logs to the evening fire, which brightened the area considerably and cast strange shadows on the surrounding cliffs. The rice water was soon boiling, as was the TVP pot, and Hall was busy mixing the pudding until all the lumps were fully dissolved and it was ready to set up. Hall sat on a rock behind the fireplace, occasionally stirring the rice and TVP while he watched the shadows dance on the cliff. It was as if the petroglyphs had come to life. Every time he looked at the cliffs, the shadows took on different forms. They looked like dancers from an earlier time. Hall finished preparing dinner, threw a few more logs on the fire, and sat down with his plate, watching the shadow dancers as he ate. He sat mesmerized by the movement, and his thoughts began to drift. Had his shadow dancers been waiting all these years for a campfire's flickering light to give them life?

It was an interesting thought, and Hall fell into an increasingly contemplative state as his mind dove deeper into the subject of real and unreal. They were echoes of the past, waiting only for a camper's fire to relive their historic glory, footprints in the cosmic memory wave that records all events, dancing for him and all who came before, thought Hall, still mesmerized by their rhythmic motion. Hall suddenly found himself standing and dancing with them. He had learned to Indian dance years before at summer camp but had never really danced outside of the camp experience. Yet the thought of why he was dancing never crossed his mind. It seemed so natural, a connection between spirit, mind, and body. As he danced between the fire and the cliff, his shadow joined the cliff dancers, and he felt a connection with them and their past. It was a sacred moment, and Hall was unaware of anything but the communion of the dance, like a whirling dervish who was suddenly lost in the ecstasy of the moment.

He awoke the next morning lying on his sleeping bag but still dressed. He felt refreshed but wondered how long he had danced with the shadows and how he had found his way to his tent and blessed sleep. Stepping outside, he noticed that the kitchen was entirely cleaned up and put away from the night before, yet he had no recollection of doing so, or even eating for that matter. He only remembered the dance. As the sun came up over the horizon and hit the cliffs, the paintings seemed somehow more vibrant, as if only recently placed there by the artist. The sun's rays bouncing off the ripples in the water seemed to reenergize the paintings, just as the flickering firelight had the evening before.

This morning was different than the others. He felt no compulsion to break camp quickly. Maybe it was the fact that his trip would soon come to an end, or maybe he had found something that he wanted to experience a little longer, something beyond the ability of words to describe, something permanent in a transient world. He took out his journal and began to write.

> Are the shadow dancers less real than I am? Surely their lives span only between each flicker of light, but if time is removed from the equation, is our existence that different? Clearly our bodies are comprised of a firmer substance than that of the shadow dancers, but again time renders us just as transient as the movements of the dancers. The question is not one of manifestation perhaps, but rather of consciousness.
>
> Is there a level of consciousness left behind by each artist in the energy imparted to his or her creation, or is it my conscious connection that gave them life? Were those depicted on the cliffs dancing in another dimension as their shadows danced in this one? Was I a shadow in their world as they were in mine? Are we all not energy waves existing everywhere and always simultaneously in a realm without time? Is someone in their time pondering the mirror image of these questions that I ponder now? Clearly this is fantasy, but like the shadows on Plato's Cave, are they the reflection of a small piece of reality? Perhaps the biggest question on my mind is, who cleaned up my campsite after dinner last night?

Hall smiled to himself as he wrote the last sentence, not sure if he really wanted an answer.

CHAPTER FIFTEEN
Two Days Remaining

Hall looked over his shoulder at the magical cliffs as he paddled out into the lake. Silently he bid them good-bye until the next time. Somehow he didn't feel like he was leaving them behind. Rather a piece of them had been lodged in his mind, never to be forgotten. He nodded at them, turned, and continued down the lake.

Mornings in the wilderness are always full of wonder—from the calm of daybreak to the breezes of midmorning and winds of afternoon. All of it was powered by the sun while being held together by nature and its life-giving water. Mother Earth, Father Sky, this is the yin and the yang of life. Life does not exist without some of each. Life thrives with a balance of both—a delicate balance that is the essence of all creation. Certainly this all didn't just happen by virtue of some grand mathematical formula or even pure chance. Most of the phylum (or categories of life) that exist today appeared in the last 50 million years. Where were they during the hundreds of millions of years previous?

It seemed that when the earth was ready, life burst forth with a vengeance. A grander cause must have been behind the evolution of creation. Somehow the world has chosen to embrace the theories of randomness, chance, and survival of the fittest, to the exclusion of spirit and consciousness. Those who over history have attempted to add spirit and consciousness to the equation have been marginalized within the walls of religion. Some were disgraced or defamed, and a few can be counted among a long list of martyrs. Nevertheless their revelations echo across the ages and are always available to those who choose to listen. Hall pondered these thoughts as he traveled down the lake.

Hall was suddenly startled out of his contemplation by a powerful and unexpected gust of wind. Looking to the sky behind him, he was surprised to see a dark front of storm clouds moving down the lake toward him. He could see the accompanying winds moving in rapid fashion toward his small canoe, along with a curtain of rain and flashes of lightning with thunder a few seconds behind. *Uh-oh,* he thought. *I've got trouble now.*

He had just enough time to strap his camping equipment securely to the canoe and put on his rain gear before the full force of the storm hit. He looked around for a protective place to weather the storm, but he was in the middle of the lake about two miles from the nearest shore.

The last place you want to be during an electrical storm is in a canoe in the middle of a lake. The alternative, under a tree on shore, was not much better, but that was Hall's only reasonable option. Hall headed for shore as quickly as he could. He felt a burst of power from a shot of adrenaline triggered by a flash of surprisingly close lightning and simultaneous echoing thunder. Hall knew he should be frightened but was too busy propelling his small boat to safety to dwell on it.

Whoa, he thought, as another flash of lightning and thunder exploded close to him. *That was too close.*

"Okay, I see you, I'm hurrying," he heard himself say as he smiled toward the heavens. Hall closed his eyes, momentarily focusing on how much he loved God's great outdoors and remembering his place as an intimate part of His creation. A feeling of peace came over him, and although still in the storm, he felt a protective kinship with it. He smiled at the wonder of nature's fury as the rain beat on his face and buffeting winds and waves did their best to change the course of his small canoe. He was no longer a mere traveler through the storm but strangely had become an intimate part of nature's tempest.

He yelled encouragement to the sky, hardly audible over the raging wind and crashing swells. "Is that all you've got, my brothers?" he shouted as he smiled at the intense communion of his circumstances. The sky flashed and thundered back.

Hall felt wonderful, thankful, and joyful; he was happy beyond description. He was intensely alive, not separate from the storm in any way but moving as a part of it. He felt a protective calm surrounding his craft, while still participating fully in the storms unpredictable energy. He thought of the Doors song, "Riders on the Storm." He was the rider on the storm. He was the storm, which through him was given a front-row seat to witness its own fury.

He thought of God experiencing His creation through His own consciousness incarnated as humankind, incarnated as Hall. Time seemed to stand still as he powered his way to shore. He pulled around a point to a spot protected from the wind, beached his canoe, and laid down on some moss looking up at the treetops bending furiously with each gust. It was a magnificent moment. Hall thought about John Muir again and his love of nature's fury. Hall always wondered about the magic that he must have experienced. Now he knew firsthand. No storm would ever be viewed the same again. The wonder of spirit and nature playing together, viewed through created consciousness anchored in man. Each piece was essential to the total mosaic of creation.

Those who think that man has no place in nature are so misguided. Those who see themselves as separate from the mysterious relationship of above and below are equally confused. It all seemed so obvious to Hall, and yet why did it take him so long to realize it? This trip had been an awakening, but how many others would be able to avail themselves of a similar opportunity? Hall knew now that he was connected to all his brothers and sisters, to all that exists. He felt an overwhelming desire to share this knowledge, but how? No one who is not ready to hear will listen. There is no verbal formula that can convey the message even to those with open ears.

Hall closed his eyes and began to drift away. A familiar voice called to him. "Quite a ride, wasn't it?"

"Joshua, where did you come from?" Hall said.

"Just another rider on the storm." Joshua smiled back. "I heard your concerns. Messages of love travel fast. You are now ready to do the work you planned before time began. I am here only to help point you in the right direction."

"Joshua, I am suddenly overcome by a desire to help lift others, who still are asleep, to this wonderful connectedness we all share, but the task seems too daunting," said Hall. "The world is totally aligned against these ideas. Its educational institutions, established scientific theories, even mainstream religions are seemingly on the other side of a vast void from these revelations. I wouldn't know where to start, how to convey these ideas, or even if I should. I'm just a small player in a canoe traveling through the wilderness. I am not a teacher or even worthy of such a reference."

"You are not the first to feel this way, nor will you be the last," said Joshua. "Many have found themselves where you now stand. Some have gone on with their lives without saying a word. Some have inadvertently started major religious movements. But all have played a role in helping raise people to a vibratory level that allows them to remember. Some teach through their words. Others teach by sharing their loving energy through example, writings, and artwork. All are equally effective."

"Knowing and living these truths is all that one needs to focus on. Khalil Gibran's, *The Prophet*, states, 'Do not try to direct love's path. Love, if it finds you worthy, directs your path.' Live these ideas and love will direct your path. Your worry is not of the spirit. It is from the mind, small m. Go live your life with the joy you have discovered and everything else will fall into place. Those who need you will find you. Those who walk next to you will recognize you and help you with your work as you help them. Often no words are spoken, but always spirit's work is being done."

"Spreading the word is not a function of speaking; it is a function of sharing energy. Everyone already knows these truths. They are indelibly inscribed on each human heart. People have just temporarily forgotten. And don't worry, remember, you are not alone. Many have already awakened, and a vast amount of energy is streaming into creation to help with the awakening process. Know that this is so and you have all the tools you need."

"But what about the institutional biases of the world that are arrayed against these ideas? How does one deal with rigid thinking, superstitious fears, and ignorance?" asked Hall.

"In a very real way these are all just illusions, as the thoughts comprising a dream are illusions," answered Joshua. "Again, you must remember that each of us already knows the truth. Just help with the awakening and the illusions will melt away, like awakening from a dream. It may appear that there are forces arrayed against you, and many of the sleepers dream a dream of power, wealth, and sustaining the status quo within which they have profited handsomely in their dream. But these too will awaken as the world's vibration is raised by workers like you, and they too will join you in your efforts. Not until all are awake is our work done. Let the truth effortlessly flow through you, and always have an unwavering trust in spirit."

With a sudden crack of thunder Hall, opened his eyes and realized he was still lying on the moss staring up at the treetops. The rain had stopped, as had the wind, and it was clear that the heart of the storm had moved down the lake. Hall looked around for Joshua, but he was not there. *Hmm*, Hall thought to himself.

CHAPTER SIXTEEN
Back to Civilization

The seaplane was scheduled to pick up Hall and bring him and his gear back to civilization at 2:00 p.m. Hall had traveled from one side of the Quetico Park to the other without seeing another human, except for Joshua, and Hall wasn't quite sure what category to put him in.

The Quetico Park is a wilderness area, and as such, planes cannot land within its boundaries. There are several ways to access the park—car, boat, canoe, or plane, but all must do so via a bordering lake and traverse the park under their own power. Motors are strictly forbidden.

Hall had camped that evening on a small island where he and the seaplane operator had agreed to meet. He had been out almost two weeks and had grown a nice beard to prove it. Looking into a small steel mirror he carried, he almost didn't recognize himself, but there was a fresh glow to his face despite almost certainly a loss of several pounds.

"I didn't need those anyway, but I might keep the mustache," he mused to himself.

He rose early that morning, wanting to enjoy the day as completely as possible. He was fully packed except for a small pack with personal items. It was nearly 10:00 a.m. and just warm enough for a swim.

Might as well, he thought, and he quickly stripped and dove into the cool water. The water was exceptionally clear, and he saw a few small fish swim by as he glided weightlessly over a small reef. The water streamed over him, cooling every inch of his body. He took a stroke and continued to glide along, now having been under water almost a minute. An ache for fresh air reminded him to surface, and he continued quietly along the shore with a gentle breaststroke. A mother duck and her brood of ducklings let Hall swim to within a few feet of them before scurrying along. Hall continued to follow them, but they stayed always a few yards ahead. He stopped and held very still, and one of the ducklings swam over to him. Thinking Hall was a log or otherwise inanimate object, the other ducklings soon joined their sibling, nestling close to Hall's chest, which was just out of water as he stood on a submerged rock. Hall barely breathed and was afraid to even blink his eyes as he watched the babies. Mom, who had continued her cruise, suddenly turned and realized she had lost something. With an authoritative quack, her brood immediately took notice and began to swim toward her.

That is, all but the first duckling, who continued to stay close to Hall's warm body. "I think I'll name you Hughie," he said, thinking of Donald Duck's mischievous nephew. Mom and the other ducks soon rounded a bend and were out of sight when Hall realized he needed to help his little friend catch back up or he might be left behind. Lowering himself gently into the water, the little duck followed Hall as he quietly swam toward the point of shoreline Hughie's family had just rounded. Surprisingly Hughie followed him. Hall's fully bearded head must have looked like a duck of sorts as he swam along.

Hall became a little concerned as he rounded the bend and didn't see Hughie's family. He searched the shore carefully. There in a thicket along the shore were his brothers and sisters, just where Mom left them when she went to search for her missing son. Mom was not far away, and when she saw Hughie following Hall, she flapped one wing and played the injured duck routine, hoping that Hall would follow, leaving her brood intact. Hall ushered Hughie into the thicket with his siblings and obligingly swam after the mother duck. She continued her injured duck act a few more times as Hall climbed out of the water and hid behind a tree, watching from a distance to make sure the little ones were okay. The mother duck soon circled back, and all were reunited. Hall walked the short distance back to camp, wondering at it all.

It is going to be tough leaving this place, he thought. He had been on many canoe trips in the past, and all were magical in their own special way. This trip, however, was especially magical—not so much because of the modified route he had chosen, for several of the lakes he had visited, he had not paddled before, but because of the different way he had experienced them. *In fact,* he thought to himself, *I wasn't a visitor at all, but rather a full participant within nature's wilderness.*

Once I crossed this threshold of understanding, nature opened up to me, revealing its secrets as if I had a right to know, as if some long-forgotten heritage was being reclaimed by me and happily granted by the balanced essence of heaven and earth that we call nature.

Hall's body tingled at the thought, and closing his eyes he found himself totally aware of all around him, yet completely empty of thought. He found himself in a place of infinite possibilities, totally still, while totally powerful. His body began to tremble, and he heard a wind in his ears. The pressure between his eyebrows began to build, and the top of his head tingled with a palpable crackle. He heard voices, laughter, and joyous singing. He was having another wakening experience. The Bible refers to it as a visitation of the Holy Spirit, while Eastern practices might call it Chi or a Kundilini awakening. This was the same experience he had had a few weeks earlier, which had compelled him to take this trip. As with the previous experience, at a certain amplitude fears began to creep in. Will I awaken? Am I dying? This time, however, he dismissed any fearful thoughts, letting them gently float by, not connecting with them in any way as he had previously done.

In a flash of insight, he suddenly could see everything around him. He was still sitting where he had always been, but all was glowing with a pulsating energy. The trees, rocks, moss, wild flowers, even his canoe looked like pure crystalline energy. He noticed that his eyes were still closed, yet he could see everything more clearly and with greater detail than had they been open. All was energy, and everything was connected. Nothing was separate. His body glowed with a special brightness. He seemed to be a human rainbow of colors, with red toward the base of the spine, then orange, yellow, green, blue, and indigo and violet around his head. Suddenly he could see himself sitting there. He had a huge smile on his face and was pulsating with color, only he was not there. He was outside his body. He saw an eagle in the sky and instantly was flying next to it. He thought of the cliff paintings of a few nights before and was instantly there, the paintings dancing more dynamically than before, but this time the light came from him. He thought of his girlfriend and could see her doing her laundry close to where each of them lived in the city. He could hear her very thoughts and realized that she loved him and missed him. He noticed that there was the most beautiful glow around her, and he realized how much he loved her too. He would see her soon.

He found himself back in the city near his apartment and watched as friends; neighbors and strangers went about their daily routine. Each had a distinctive light signature. All were beautiful, but some glowed more brightly than others. He saw Alice, his neighbor, whose light barely glowed at all and heard her say in her thoughts how much she missed her son who had died in a motorcycle accident, which she felt was her fault, as she had consented to his buying the bike. The glow from her heart area was almost nonexistent since she had lost her love and couldn't love herself through the guilt. Hall was moved by her pain, a pain that was so unnecessary. Hall then saw her son standing next to her, although she couldn't see him, unable to move on because of his own guilt from leaving her alone.

Hall saw many that glowed so brightly that he felt at any moment they would burst from their chains and join him in the work Joshua had described. Just the right word, just the right circumstance, and they would be free. He saw others who had chosen through their ignorance to restrict or even shut down their glow. Their self-imposed chains called to Hall. He now knew where his future lay. He now knew what he was to do. With a thought that he was ready to work, with a thought of compassion, love, and connectedness to all of creation, he suddenly found himself back in his body on the island in Canada's Quetico Park. He heard a seaplane overhead, opened his eyes, and gave thanks. He was ready.

CHAPTER SEVENTEEN
Heading Home

The drone of the seaplane engine was hypnotic as Hall looked out the window of the De Havilland Beaver that had picked him up. Looking down, he saw the tip of his canoe tied to the De Havilland's strut just above the right float. It had been his reliable companion for the last two weeks. It had ferried him through nature's peace and fury, and he would miss it when he finally left for home.

Miles and miles of forest seemingly stretching forever, interspersed with clear lakes, rivers, streams, and granite outcroppings, presented a feast for Hall's eyes. Most of the bodies of water were connected, either by some waterway, river, or beaver stream, a huge drainage system still showing clear signs of the last passing glacier.

Looking out over nature's breathtaking tapestry, a flashing glint caught Hall's eye. As the plane traveled closer, he could see the flashing came from a particularly beautiful lake situated on a high plateau. It was a deep turquoise blue, like that of a special diamond. It was a jewel among jewels. As the plane got closer, the lake seemed to be unconnected to those around it. There were no obvious rivers or streams flowing into the lake and none flowing out. The water was a deep turquoise blue, and as the plane flew by,

Hall could see its crystal clear waters changed from blue green along the shore to a deep indigo blue in the center. This was a very, very deep lake. Hall couldn't take his eyes off of it.

It must be spring fed, Hall thought, for usually isolated lakes, which lacked fresh circulating water, were somewhat stagnant. This lake was too pristine, too pure. Hall wondered if man had traveled to the lake, for it clearly was not part of a connective waterway. He strained to find some evidence of runoff. Clearly there was substantial circulation taking place. Springs could explain the source of fresh water coming in, but there was no evidence of water flowing out.

It was a perplexing mystery. *There must be an underground waterway,* he thought. A few miles south, he got his answer.

There gushing from the side of a cliff was a large waterfall. The water was crystal clear and in the sunlight had the same turquoise color Hall had seen at the mysterious lake. There was no obvious stream leading to the falls. Perhaps it was underground. It must be connected. Hall wondered at how such a beautiful lake could be so hidden. What secrets did it hold, and why was he so consumed by it?

Raising his voice over the droning engines, he asked his pilot, Erik, if he knew anything about his mystery lake. Erik was a classic-looking grizzled bush pilot. He had been flying seaplanes in various Canadian and Alaskan wilderness areas for over thirty years. His weathered skin told of years in nature, and his face expressed a firmness of resolve, yet an undeniable kindness. Erik, who had spoken less than two or three words since the pickup, looked long and hard at Hall with a studying concentration. Looking back at his instruments and flight path, he was silent for a long time. Hall thought that perhaps he was unable to hear him over the engines and considered rephrasing his question. But he could see that Erik was far off in thought and decided not to ask again.

Lost in his own thoughts about the beautiful lake, Hall was somewhat startled when Erik turned to him and responded, "That lake is a special one, Hall. Only a few are aware of it. It is sacred to the Indians and difficult to get to. Just as its waters flow in and out from unknown waterways, so entrance to the lake and its mystery can only be obtained by a few. Rarely do my passengers even notice it as we fly by. The Indians say that it is constantly singing a song to passersby, a song that only a few can hear. They say that those who hear it are compelled to come to it and drink its waters. You have heard it, Hall, so if the legend is correct, I will see you again." He paused and then added, "But then again, it is only a legend."

With that comment, Erik became quiet again. In the short time that Hall was with him, he felt a certain kinship, although to his knowledge they had never met. There was something more about this man, some secret. Hall felt that someday their paths would cross again.

Hall took out his map and marked the mysterious lake. "Someday," he said to himself. "Someday."

TO BE CONTINUED

www.ingramcontent.com/pod-product-compliance
Lightning Source LLC
Chambersburg PA
CBHW071900070526
44583CB00016B/1774